THE A TO Z BOOK OF MUSHROOMS

A Beginner's Guide

By Michael P. Earney

Copyright Michael P. Earney 2019 All Rights Reserved.

No part of this book may be reproduced, stored in a retrieval system, or transmitted by any means, electronic, mechanical, photocopying, recording, or otherwise, without written permission from the author.

ISBN-13: 978-1-941345-72-6   HB

ISBN-13: 978-1-941345-73-3   PB

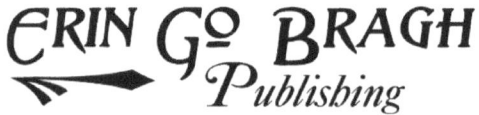

Canyon Lake, TX
www.ErinGoBraghPublishing.com

Cover Illustration

Clathrus archerii, Octopus stinkhorn, Devil's fingers. Native to Australia and Tasmania, *C. archerii* also known as, *Anthurus archerii,* was unwittingly shipped to California and has also made its way to Asia and Europe.

Acknowledgments

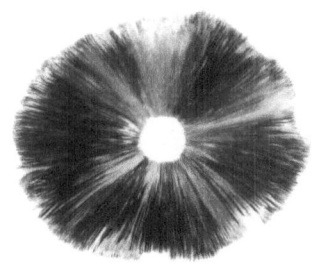

Thanks to family and friends who have encouraged and supported me in this effort.

A special thanks to Kathleen J. Shields for her graphic design and publishing skills.

Disclaimer

The information in this book is accurate to the best of the authors knowledge. It is intended for educational purposes only. Always consult the most professional sources available before consuming wild mushrooms.

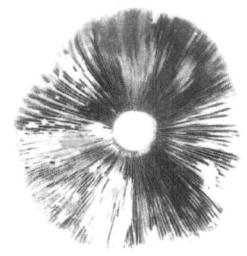

For Mushrooms

The words fungi and mushroom don't roll off the tongue
They're smelly, they're nasty, they grow mostly on dung!
At least, that's the perception some people hold.
To eat a wild mushroom, you have to be bold
Or stupid, or crazy, those people would say.
It grew in the woods? You should throw it away!
If only they knew what you and I know,
They'd be out there seeking to find where they grow.
Once hooked on the mushroom, you never go back.
For breakfast, lunch, dinner, or just a quick snack
They're delicious, medicinal, and magical too!
In their hundreds, their thousands, or only a few.
You seek under ledges, wade grass to the knees,
You jump over fences and start to climb trees.
Although there are many you may never see,
Do get to know those that it's best to let be.
Their names, familiar, now roll off the tongue
Shaggy Mane, Chanterelle — and those growing on dung.

Michael P. Earney 2018

THE A TO Z BOOK OF MUSHROOMS

A Beginner's Guide

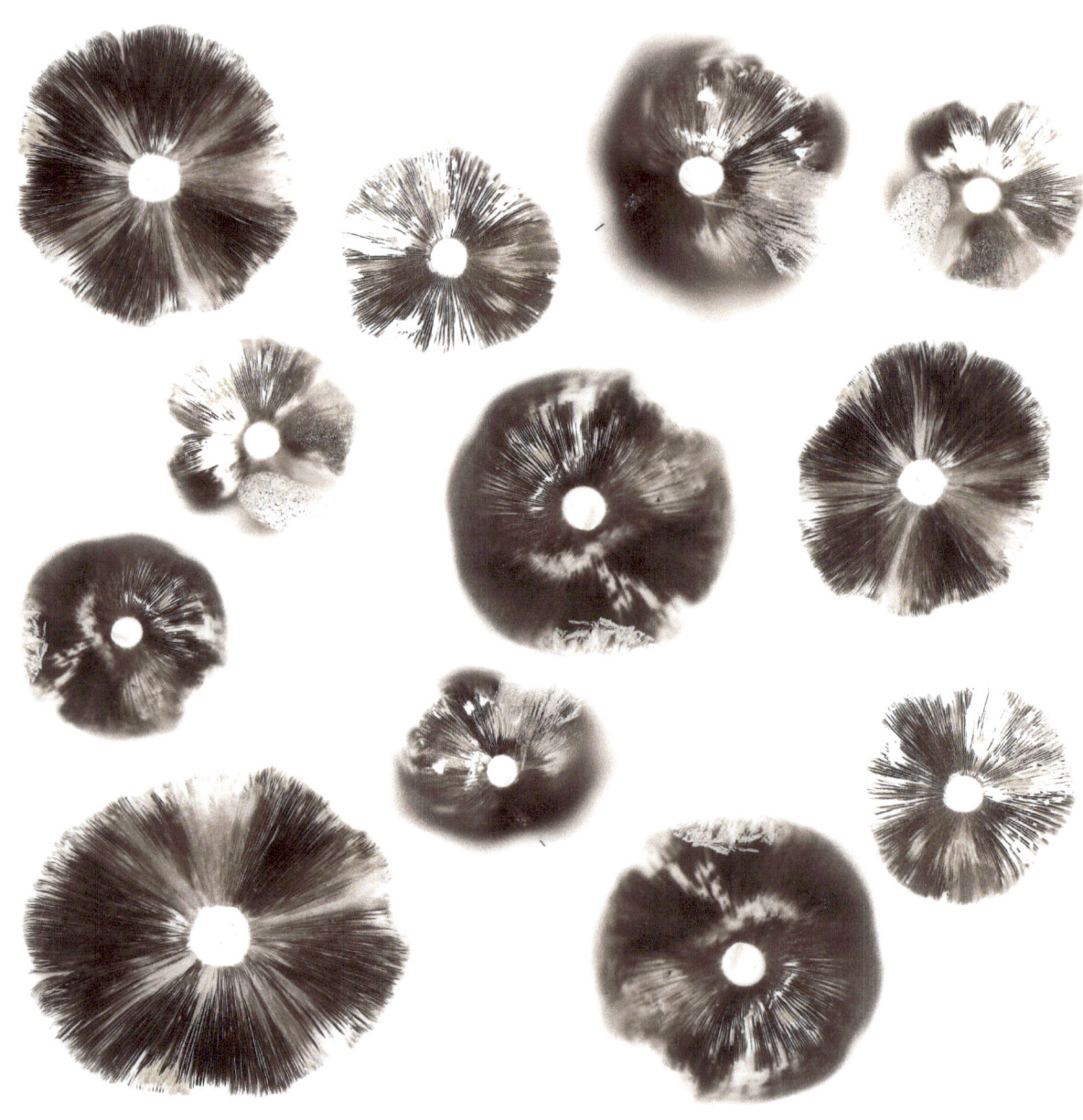

Introduction

For most of us, the image we see when we think of a mushroom is the white button or those Portobello mushrooms we find in the produce department at the local store; a stem, a cap (stipe and pileus to a mycologist), and gills under the cap. If only it were that simple! Mushrooms, sometimes called toadstools (we'll come to that later), take some of the most incredible shapes, sizes and colors imaginable. The word, mushroom can be applied to almost any fungus that forms a fruiting body. The fruiting body is the fleshy, above ground, spore bearing thing that pops up from under the soil or on its food source, which is very often cow poop. In one way or another, rot and decay are usually involved. This is perhaps why many people want nothing to do with mushrooms. Though they provide only small amounts of potassium, vitamin C, D, B6, Iron, Magnesium and Selenium, mushrooms are high in antioxidants. Antioxidant chemicals rid the body of the free radicals that can harm the body's cells and potentially lead to cancer. Selenium, which prevents inflammation and decreases tumor growth, together with the vitamins and folate in mushrooms, can play a significant part in preventing the formation of cancer cells. The vitamin D content can even be increased by exposing freshly cut mushrooms to direct sunlight or UV light. Vegans may be happy to know that mushrooms are the source of vitamin B12 that they can't find in plants. The medicinal and nutritional benefits that mushrooms have to offer are really quite astounding, but first we have to find them and identify them correctly.

The characteristics that enable mycologists (botanists who study fungi) to identify mushrooms are numerous. Equip yourself with as many of the available aids as you can, including a mycologist if possible, before mushroom hunting and refer to them when you return with your prize. Learning the spore pattern by placing a mushroom on a piece of paper overnight is always a helpful tool. The spore formation and color will tell you a lot. Here, however, we will primarily concentrate on the simple, outward appearance of the mushroom as it is encountered in the wild. There are several distinguishing features in mushrooms. These are; color, shape, size and often, location. All are very useful clues to note. Shelf mushrooms grow on trees, for example. Some mushrooms like open spaces, others grow in the shade of specific trees with which they have a symbiotic relationship. The more common mushrooms can easily be identified by these means and each of the illustrated mushrooms will have the immediate things to look for in the accompanying text, plus further aids that can be carried out once you get home. It can't be stressed too strongly that, just like anything else found in the wild, whether it is an animal, vegetable or mineral, be very careful when handling, smelling or eating mushrooms you find. This goes for even those you may be confident you know. Familiarity breeds contempt, as they say, and there are always those who become sick or die from over-confidence, misidentification or recklessness. Also, you never know what you might be allergic to. Take a bag or two to keep different species separate, a basket is good to have should you find a lot, a knife (cutting mushrooms rather than pulling them up is recommended, though the base of the mushroom may need to be looked at as another means of identification), a pair of gloves, and a trusted mushroom guide book. If you can go with a dedicated mushroom hunter, so much the better. But don't be put off by all these warnings, the last thing I want to do is to dissuade anyone from gathering mushrooms. If you find you really enjoy the activity, you are not alone. Mycophilia (myco, "fungus", philos, "loving") is more common than you might think. In fact, it can become an obsession. There are groups, clubs, societies, experts and amateurs who will, at the slightest hint of rain, head out to their favorite hunting grounds or to the new and unknown. There are festivals, conferences, organized forays and hunting championships that can attract hundreds or thousands of mushroom fans and innumerable websites. You might travel the world in search of that one elusive mushroom to add to your list. There are 1.5 million species of fungi, a mere five percent of which have been identified. Not all produce fruiting bodies you would be interested in, but if you wanted to have a fungus named for you, the opportunity is there. Whether hunting in a group or heading out on your own, whether the hunt is successful or not, you will want to do it again. I guarantee.

I think it is one of the great delights of life to experience the thrill of coming upon nature's bounty in the form of the mushroom. To be able to identify, pick, cook and eat them adds another dimension to the joy of living. Going from A to Z means that I will show you many members of the fungi world that you may never encounter in the wild but will, I hope, enjoy seeing and reading about.

Michael P. Earney 3/19/2018

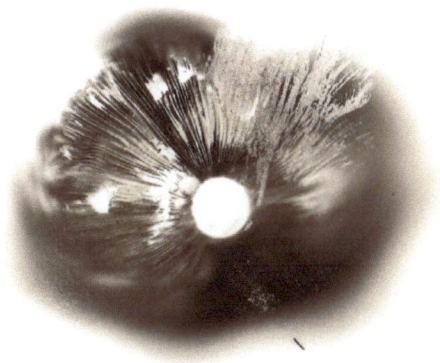

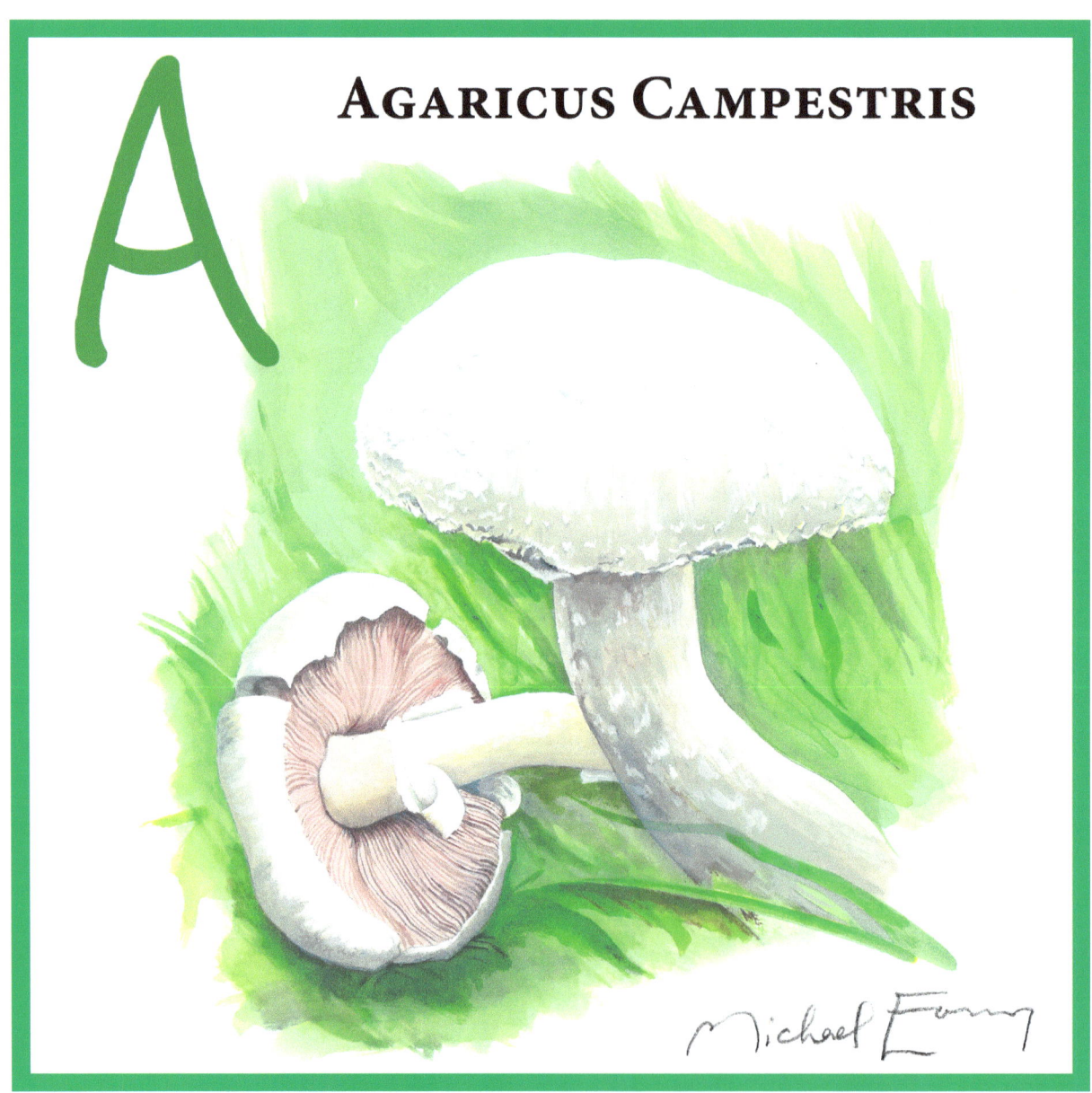

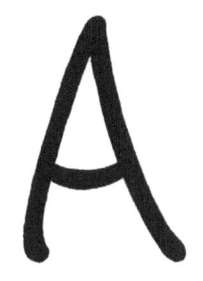**A** is for **Agaricus Psalliota**

Agaricus bisporous is the dominant cultivated mushroom in the USA. It's called the common mushroom, because it's common, but it's also known as the button mushroom. It's the one you find in the grocery store. Along with the field mushroom (*Agaricus campestris*), shown here, and the Horse mushroom (*A. arvensis*), it's the most widely recognized. Unlike the button, the other two can be found in the wild. They all have the white domed cap that flattens as it grows. The older ones will have brown flakes on the top, white stem and the distinctive pink gills that darken with age until they are black. I'm sure you've found some like that in the back of the refrigerator. As the names imply, they come up in fields, meadows and grassy places. Just to spoil things there is *A. xanthodermus* that you might see in the grass verge at the side of the road. Hold on, though. If it stains bright yellow, particularly near the base of the stem, you've found the Yellow Stainer, (xantodermus means, yellow-skin.) It's not deadly but it will give you an upset stomach. The Horse mushroom will bruise a little yellow but nothing like the Stainer. Just like most other species, there are the edible and those you definitely do not want to eat. Check your field guide and do a spore cast. This is an easy one, but you still need to proceed with caution. Once you know the signs to look for you can be confident. Not before. The *Agaricus blazei* comes from Brazil and is used as a medicine for a number of ailments including, cancer, type2 diabetes, osteoporosis and high cholesterol.

Cool fact: The Portabello mushroom is often bought as a special treat for the more adventurous shopper. Actually, it's *A. bisporous*, our good old button mushroom, that's been allowed to grow and age.

What other mushrooms start with A?

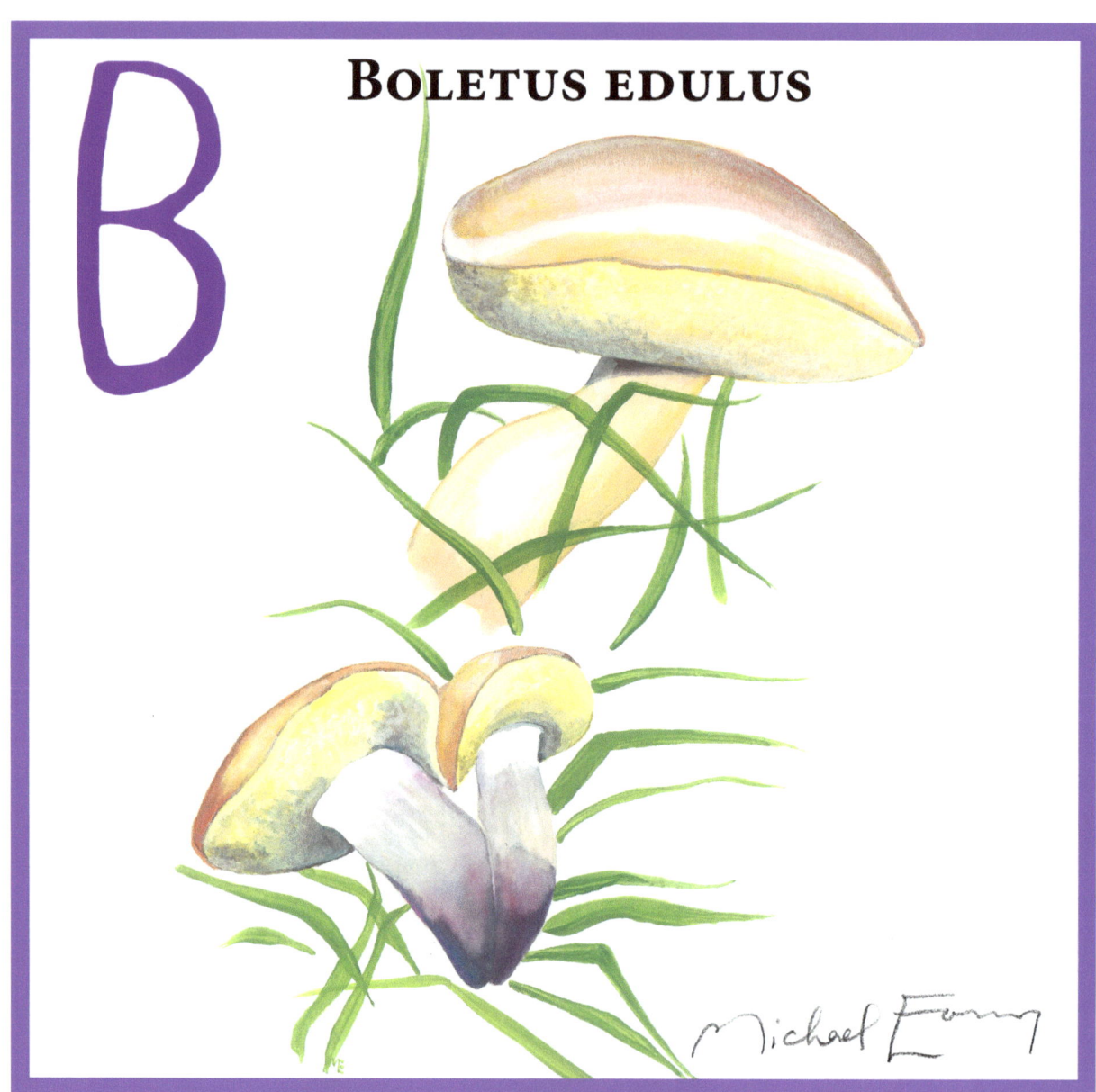

B is for **Boletus**, *Boletus edulus,* Penny bun, Porcini

Boletes were described by Swedish botanist, physician and zoologist Carl Linnaeus (1707-1778) as being all those fungi having pores. Turned out over 300 species didn't belong there. Once they were removed over 100 species of *Boletus* remained. The name comes from Ancient Greek, bōles – "lump" or "clod" which the cap can resemble when the mushroom doesn't completely push all the way through the leaves or pine needles on the ground. Keep an eye out for those, or else you might miss one of the most common edible mushrooms. Sliced and dried, they will provide good eating throughout the year. The stem will be thick and bulbous at the bottom, the cap reddish to brown, smooth and may be sticky when young. The underneath of the cap is the give-away. Instead of the gills found in most capped mushrooms, boletes have a smooth surface, from white in some, to tan or reddish brown, covered in tiny pores. These pores are the ends of tubes that contain the spores. Many boletes bruise blue when touched or cut. Those with red or orange undersides and bruise blue the quickest are considered suspect for eating. If not harvested early, bolete stems will likely have maggots in them, just discard those and keep the cap. Some boletes can grow to 14 inches across, but 4 inches is more common.

Cool fact: Carl Linnaeus laid the foundation for taxonomy, the modern system of classifying organisms. Naming taxa in ways that he thought made sense, human beings became *Homo sapiens,* "wise men". Creatures that had breasts he grouped under "mammalia" because he wanted to encourage mothers to breast feed their babies.

What other mushrooms start with B?

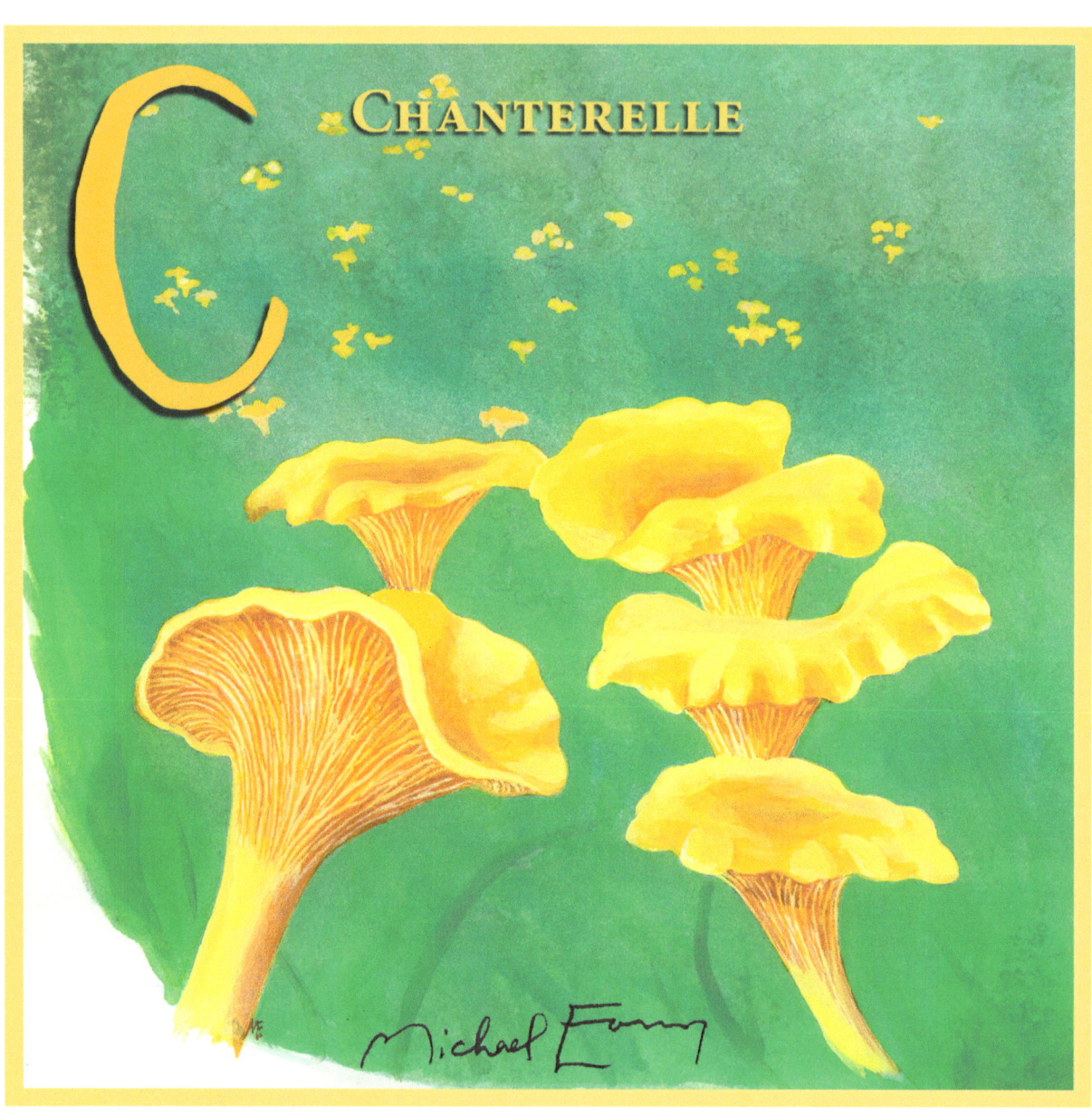

C is for **Chanterelle**, *Cantharellus cibarius* and related species

Chanterelle mushrooms have been called one of the best edible mushrooms. They are extremely nutritious and provide vitamins and minerals like most mushrooms, and are one of the richest known sources of vitamin D. Chanterelles can have a long growing season if there is rain; from late spring to early fall. They can be very prolific, so you might want to take a basket along with your knife, gloves and a brush for cleaning the chanterelles, as they can get pretty gritty. Their funnel shaped cap and the gills (called false gills as they are forked, more like ridges) that go well down the stem, are natural receptacles for dirt. They are one of the mushrooms you may need to gently wash. They can be 5" in diameter, 2" is the average size. They stay fresh for about 10 days. If you can't eat them right-away, refrigerate them in a paper bag, not plastic. They grow, often abundantly, out in the woods, looking like golden flowers, (there are white, black and peach-like relatives that are equally tasty), and they can be dried or frozen. Chanterelles can be confused with the Jack O' Lantern which you don't want to eat. Unlike chanterelles, Jack o' Lanterns grow in clumps on trees or logs while the chanterelle grows in the soil. Chanterelles are one of the more easily identified of mushrooms.

Chaga *Inonotus obliquus,* known as the "King of Medicinal Mushrooms," grows mostly on birch trees. A black, unattractive, hard, cracked exterior hides a yellowish-brown interior. Chunks of this fungus are typically brewed in hot water or alcohol and drunk as a cure for a wide range of health problems. Go to draxe.com for more information.

Cool fact: Once dried, the chanterelle doesn't reconstitute that well but can be ground into a powder to be used as a flavoring added to food or for making chanterelle flavored oil, vinegar or liquor.

What other mushrooms start with C?

D Death Cap

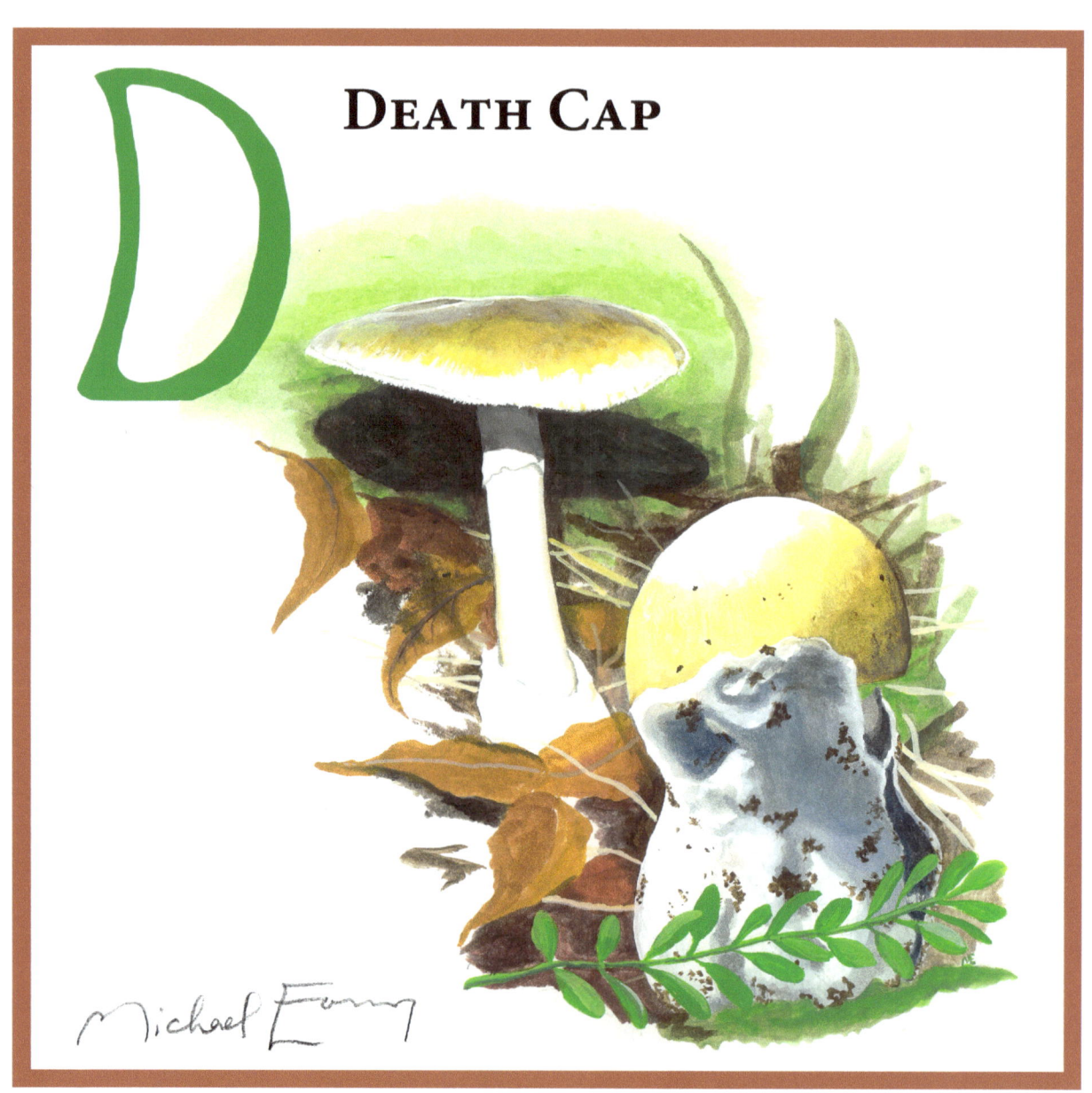

D is for **Death Cap** *Amanita phalloides, A. virosa,* Destroying Angel, *A. ocreata* also known as the Destroying angel.

Death Cap. Destroying Angel. That should tell you all you need to know about these mushrooms. They're responsible for most mushroom deaths around the world. Half a cap will do the job. These *Amanita*, especially when still covered by or just emerging from the universal veil, can resemble a puffball or a young Agaricus. Do you remember that under A you were advised to check for the color of the gills? If they are not pink, drop it right away. Unfortunately, though they are not found growing in the same location, they can be mistaken for the paddy straw mushroom, *Volvariella volvacea*, which is edible and for some of the edible *Russula* mushrooms. Note the white gills, the partial veil around the stem, the remains of the volva you will find at the bulbous base of the stem. All there? You found a death cap or a destroying angel. The *Amanita ceasarea* is a highly sought-after edible member of the genus. While it resembles the other amanitas in some regards, it has an orange cap, yellow gills and yellowish stem. All of the amanitas need to be handled with care, it's easy to make a mistake and risky to experiment. Under F, we will examine that other member of the family, *Amanita muscaria*, easily the most iconic of all mushrooms.

Cool fact: A favorite of early Roman Empire rulers, *Amanita caesarea* was named by Giovanni Antonio Scopoli (1723-1788) an Italian naturalist who shared his research and findings with Carl Linnaeus. Though they never met, Linnaeus greatly respected Scopoli's work and named a plant for him, the *Scopolia carniolica* which is used as a stomach remedy in small doses but has hallucinogenic affects in high doses.

What other mushrooms start with D?

E Ears

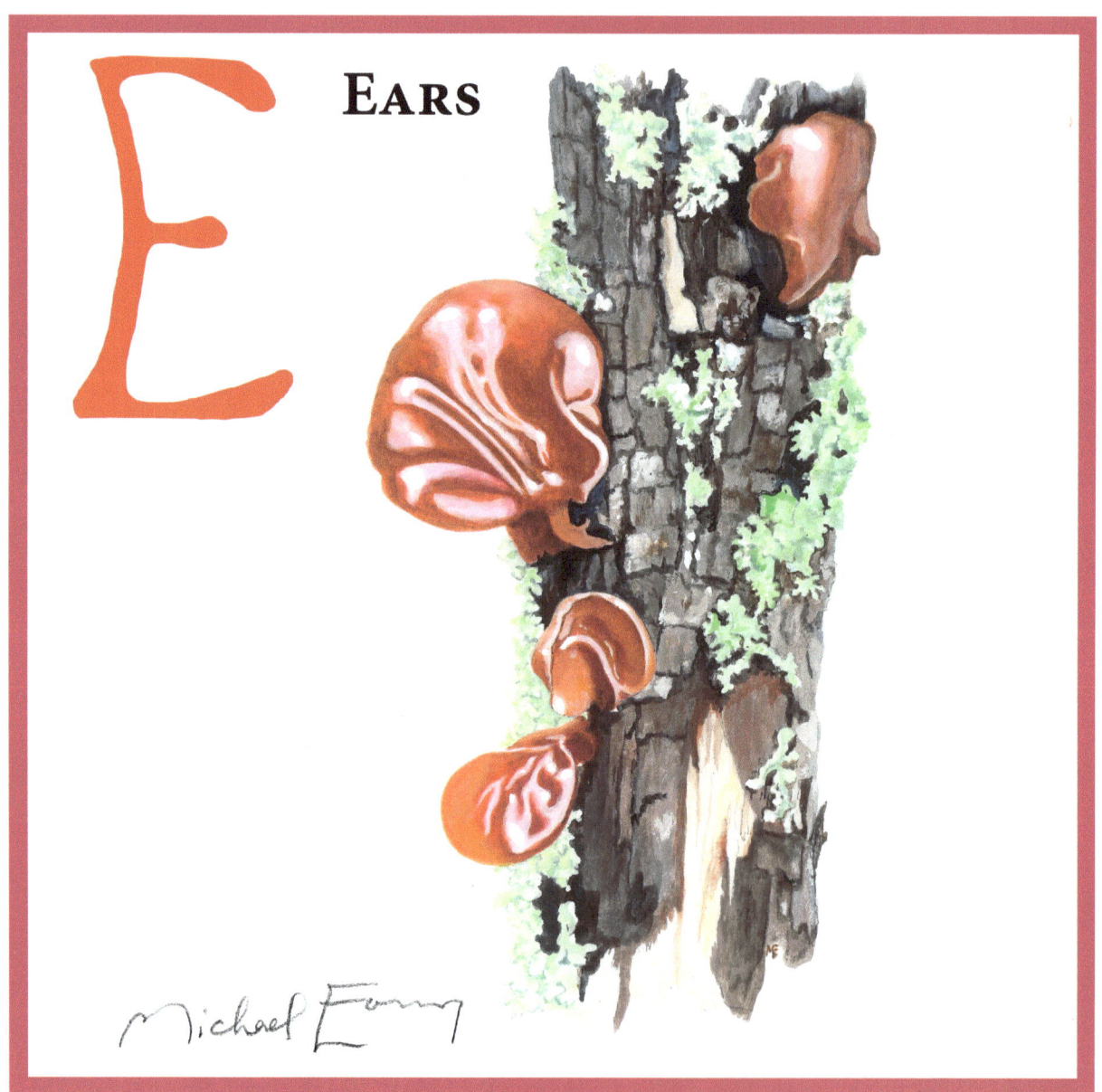

E is for **Ears**. Wood ears, tree ears, cloud ears, jelly ears, *Auricularia auricula*

Ears. Why ears? Because they look like ears and they feel like ears. Commonly known as tree ears or wood ears because they grow on dead or dying trees, these thin, purplish, grayish, brown fungi can be found pretty much year-round after rain. They dry up but flesh out again with rain, so they seem to suddenly appear, the way many other mushrooms do, out of nowhere. There are no other mushrooms that really look like them; spore casts can be made to confirm you have the right thing and consult your field guide, human or technical. There is essentially no stem, just pull them off, take them home, rinse and cook. For all that floppy, rubbery feel they are surprisingly crunchy. Popular in Asian cooking, black fungus, another name for tree ears, can be found dried, in Asian food stores. They are said to be the first cultivated mushroom, starting around 600BCE. Though not recom-mended, they can be eaten raw; there is very little taste, their appeal is more textural than visceral. What they deliver in the way of health benefits is where they shine. One cup of these guys provides more than half the recommended dietary intake of protein and dietary fiber, 9-21 percent of the daily recommended intake of iron, and lots of Vitamin B-2. Tree ears have been used in Chinese medicine for thousands of years.

Cool fact: Elephant Ear Mushroom Coral, *Rhodactis mussoides* is one of several aquatic mushrooms that are skeleton-less coral. The short tentacles on its upper surface contain toxins. It is carnivorous, feeding on small fish and crustaceans.

What other mushrooms start with E?

F   **Fly Agaric**

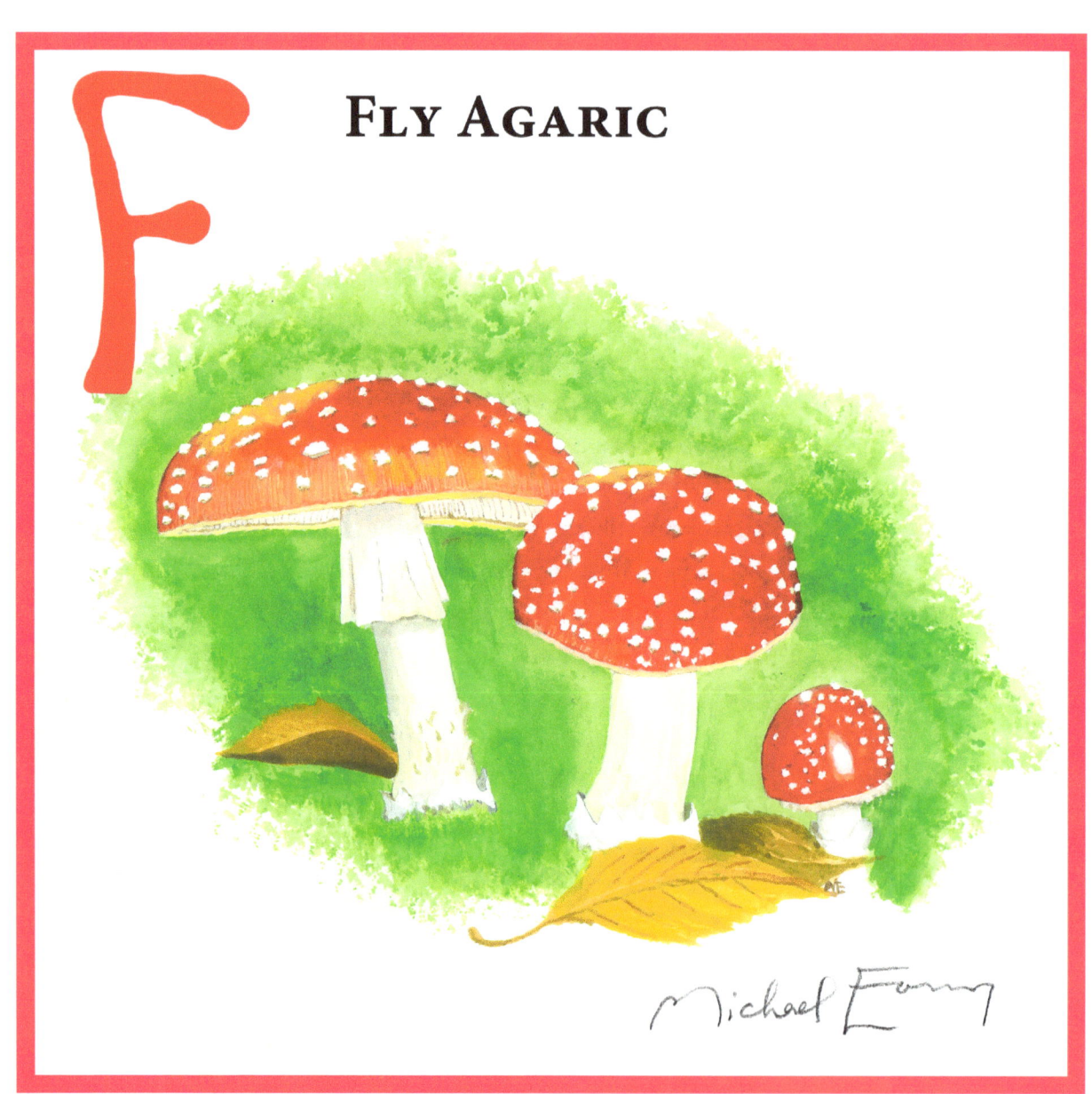

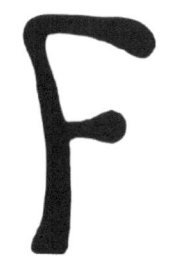 is for **Fly Agaric**, *Amanita muscaria*

Fly agaric is *the* most recognizable mushroom and the one most commonly called toadstool, having been associated with gnomes, fairies and toads in early times. Its bright red cap, sprinkled with white warts or flakes, makes it stand out in the forests where it lives. Originating in northern forests, it has spread into many southern hemisphere countries. Those white flakes are the remains of the universal veil that covers the egg-like cap as it first appears above ground. The partial veil, while attached to the cap, keeps the spores safe until they are ready to disperse. Once that happens, its remains form a ring on the stalk. The cap grows from 3 to 8 in. or bigger in diameter. Note also, the bulbous base and its remains of the veil. There are 3 subspecies that have yellow caps. In spite of its distinctive features, fly agaric can be mistaken for other yellow and red mushrooms, so the usual warnings apply. More importantly perhaps, is the fact that while its toxicity is well known, ways have been found to make it edible; par-boiling seems to be the preferred method. Various indigenous groups around the world have employed *A. muscaria* for religious ceremonies since very early times. In eastern Siberia, the shaman takes the mushroom, the psychoactive elements passing through his body unchanged. Then the other participants drink his urine. Laplanders have another method for screening out the harmful toxins: they feed the mushrooms to their reindeer first. Is that why Santa's reindeer can fly?

Cool fact: In Lewis Carroll's *Alice's Adventures in Wonderland,* the mushroom, one side of which makes her grow tall and the other that makes her short, is thought to be a reference to *A. muscaria*.

What other mushrooms start with F?

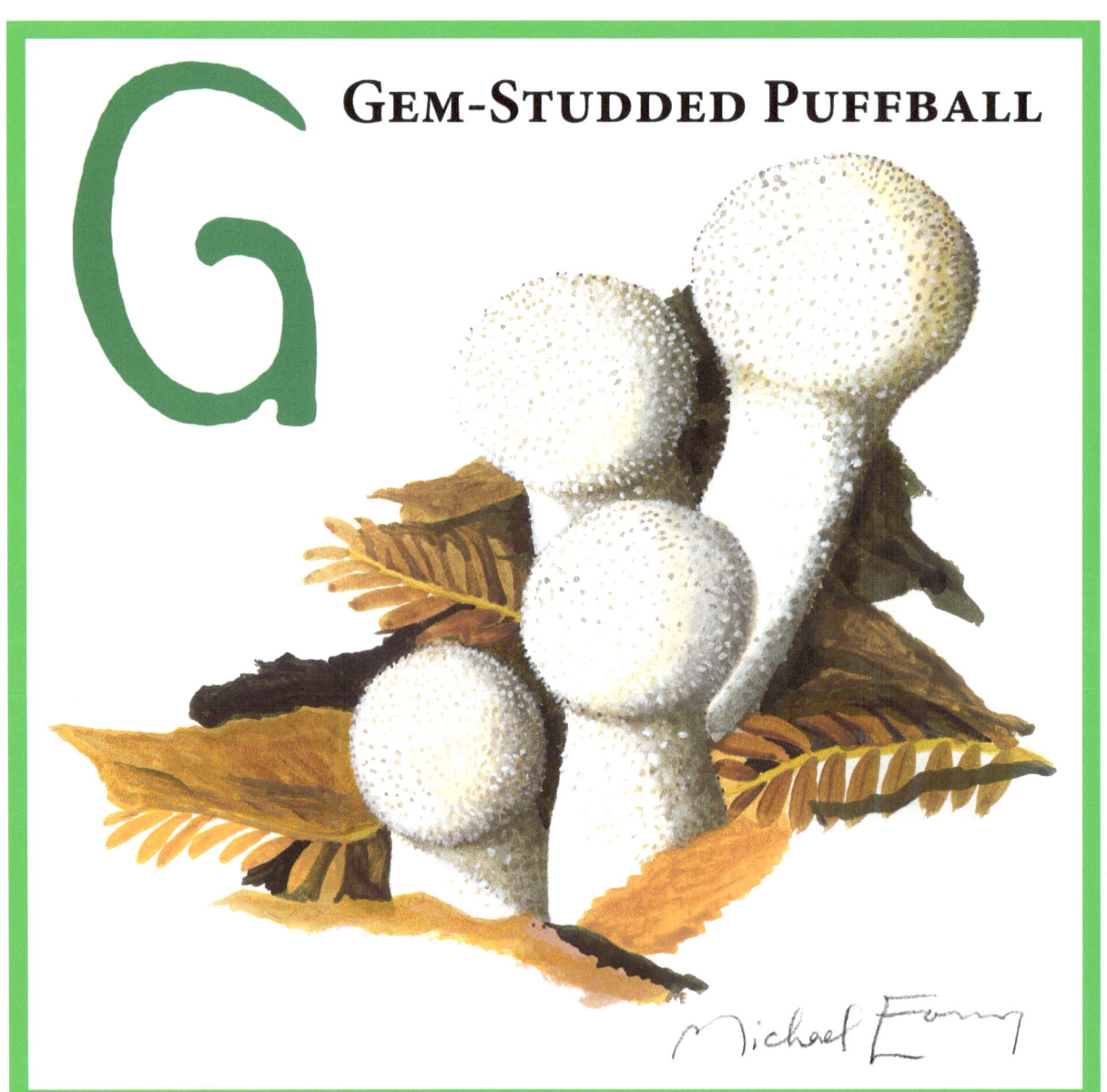

G

Gem-Studded Puffball

G is for **Gem-Studded Puffball**, *Lycoperdon perlatum*, warted puffball, devil's snuff-box

Gem-Studded Puffballs are the most common puffball, ranging from Alaska to Mexico and around the world. They are sufficiently different in appearance from the giant puffball to warrant their own space. Unlike its stemless relative, the gem-studded has a thick stalk that bulges out toward the top and forms a dome. The short spiny bumps on the dome taper down the stalk. These are the 'gems'. You will find many of them growing together, averaging two inches wide by three inches tall. The gem is a good edible when young, as the flesh is white and firm inside. Most of what is written about the giant puffball applies to the gem. They become brown and dry as they age, this is when the ostiole, the hole at the top, opens and the spores are released. Avoid inhaling the spore as it can cause respiratory problems. It's also best to avoid those growing alongside the road as they are bio-accumulators: they take up heavy metals and mercury from the soil. Like the oyster mushroom, it is being tested as a low cost, renewable material for the treatment of water and waste water. The gem-studded puffball bears some resemblance to other puffballs, but once you are familiar with it you are unlikely to confuse them. The Earthball is also similar, but cut in half, it reveals its purple, black interior, not for eating. As always, err on the side of caution.

Cool fact: *Lycoperdon*, Lycos is Greek for wolf, *perdon* comes from the Greek, *perdesthai* which derives from the Sanskrit for "to break wind", giving us "Wolf's fart", presumably referring to the brown spore that the Gem-Studded Puffball emits.

What other mushrooms start with G?

H

Hen of the Woods

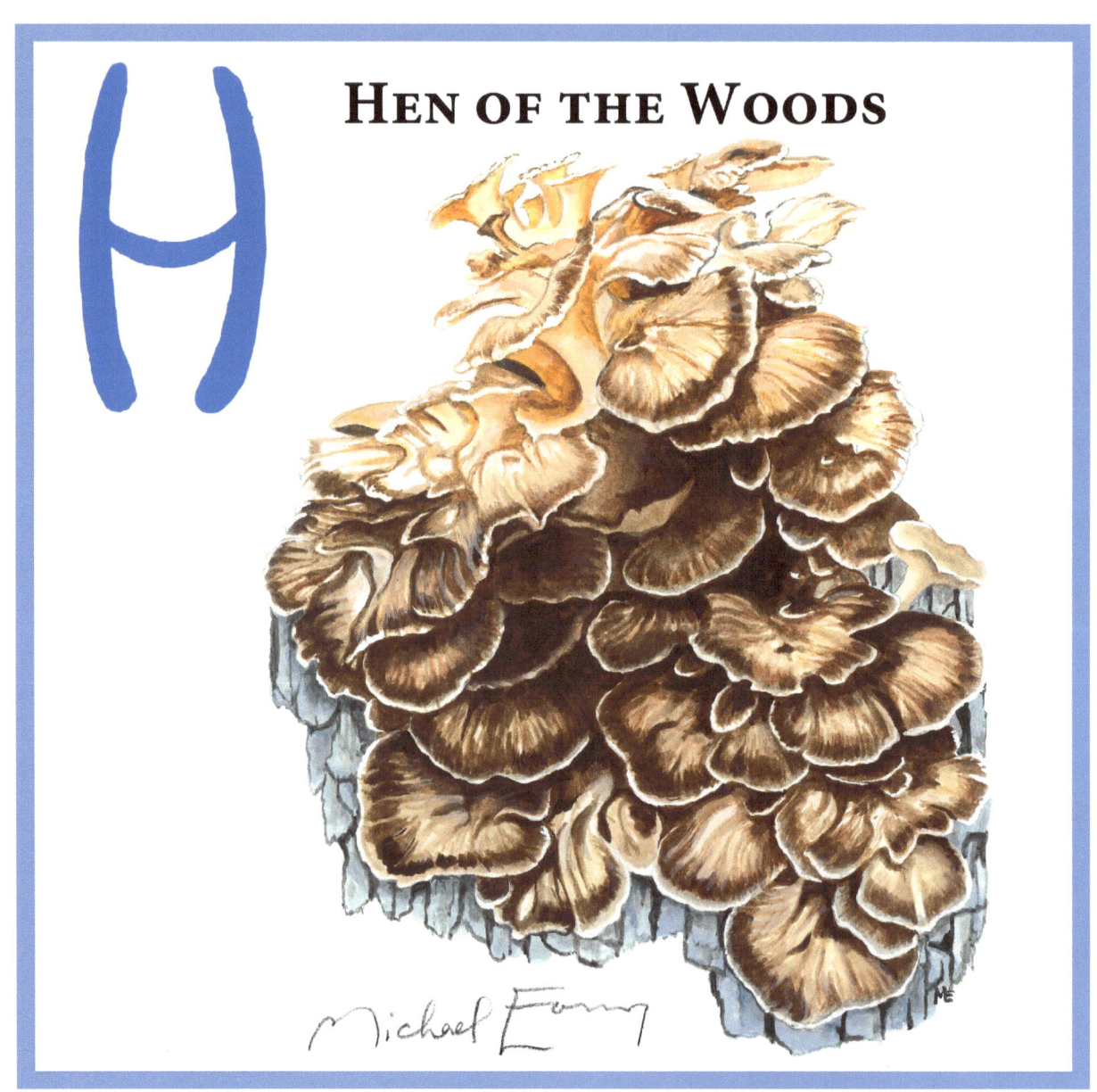

H is for **Hen of the Woods**, *Grifola frondosa,* Maitake

Hen of the Woods makes its appearance in the fall. You will only find them east of the Rockies growing at the base of dead or dying oaks or maples. They can get as big as 40lbs, but you will be happy whatever size because they taste great. They vary in color from pure white to tan, then brown to gray as they age. The clustered, darker edged petal or leaf-like overlapping fronds are anything from a half inch to two inches across. They grow to full size over a week or two, so just keep monitoring any you find, and you'll have a real prize. In Japan, where it is called Maitake, "dancing mushroom" and known as the "King of mushrooms", the Hen of the Woods can grow to more than 100 lbs.

Honey Mushroom

H is for honey mushroom *Armillaria*

Honey mushrooms are considered to be one of the best edible mushrooms in many parts of Europe. However, they must be cooked thoroughly as they are mildly poisonous when raw. In England, one species of honey mushroom can make you sick if you drink alcohol 12 hours before or 24 hours after eating them. Very often, the *Galerina* spp. will be found growing alongside the *Armillaria* spp. on the same log. The *Galerina* is fatally poisonous, so once again, do your homework and be very careful. Some Armillaria are bioluminescent.

Cool fact: The largest organism in the world is a honey mushroom, *Armillaria ostoyae,* growing in the Malheur National Forest in Oregon. It covers at least 3.4 sq. miles, is more than 2,400 years old and could be 8,350 years, which would also make it the oldest living organism in the world.

What other mushrooms start with H?

I   Inky Cap

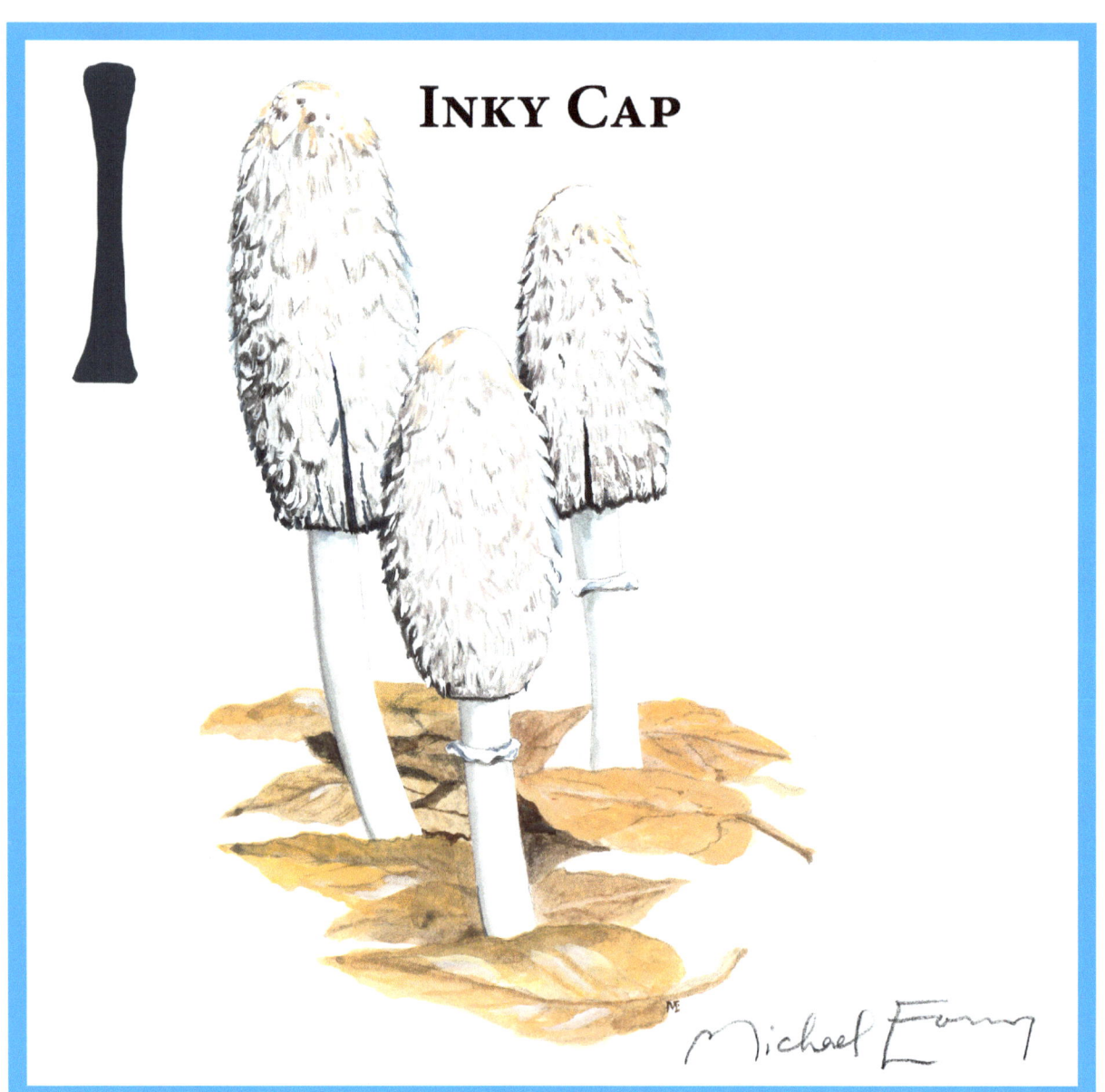

Michael Emry

I is for **Inky Cap**, *Coprinopsis atramentaria,* Ink cap, Alcohol ink cap

Inky caps are in the *Agaricaceae* family, which includes the field and button mushrooms. A common, edible when young, small, gilled mushroom with a smooth, greyish, white, turning brown cap, white stalk and gills. It's another of those mushrooms that don't go well with alcohol. In fact, if you take a drink every day, it's best that you don't eat inky caps. Even up to five days after your last drink they can cause really unpleasant reactions. You know what? If you drink at all, you should leave inky caps alone. Shaggy manes, *C. comatus*, which are equally abundant, bigger and more easily identified are the way to go. With its missile or bullet shaped flaky cap, some getting as tall as six inches, and its slim white stalk with an annular ring, the shaggy mane will satisfy any appetite. They satisfy theirs with nematodes, just like the oyster mushroom. You'll find them in the woods along with the common and the mica cap, another edible ink cap with a good flavor. All of the ink caps need to be cooked right away. If you can't eat them immediately, they can be refrigerated or frozen. In as little as 24 hrs. they will open, the edges turn up and the gills turn black as it starts to autodigest. As it eats itself the spores are released. You can find plenty of sites through Google or on Youtube that will show you how to identify, harvest and cook inky caps but don't forget to keep your field guide handy and whenever possible, go with an experienced forager.

Cool fact: In 2017, a fossilized agaricus mushroom, given the name *Gonwanagaricites magnificus,* was found in Brazil. At 125 million to 113 million years old, it's the oldest known.

What other mushrooms start with I?

J Jellied False Coral

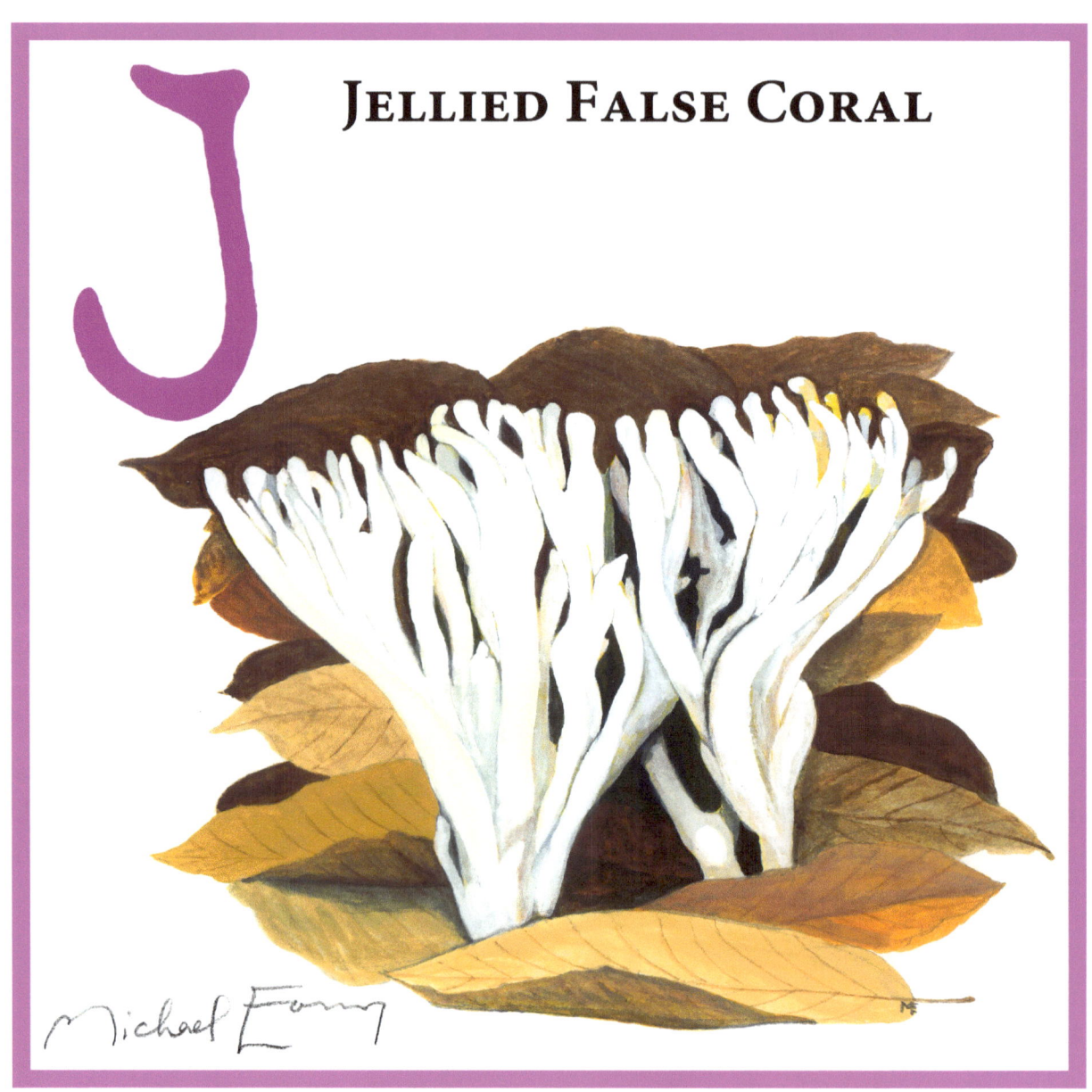

J is for **Jellied False Coral**, Tremellodendron pallidum or T. schweinitzii

Jellied False Coral gets its name from the fact that it looks like coral, is a jelly fungus and is called false because it's not really a "coral mushroom". The experts can't agree about its Latin name either, hence the two versions above. Some coral mushrooms are very tasty, although the Jellied False Coral is edible it's not worth eating. It starts out as small irregular lumps on the ground and grows very slowly until it is about 2-6inches across and 1-4inches high. Although related to the wood ear and witch's butter, it is tough and leathery. Starting out white, it turns darker as it ages and will pick up colors from the substrate upon which it is growing. It is found east of the Great Plains from Canada to Texas and on down into Mexico. So, why should you care? If you are at all interested in mushrooms it's another member of the family and should you come upon one, someday you can say; "I saw a Jellied False Coral mushroom today." That's bound to impress someone.

Cool fact: Unlike the honey mushroom and other parasitic mushrooms that slowly kill the trees among which they live, the jellied false coral is mycorrhizal, which means that its relationship with the plants around it is beneficial to both. The fungus and the rootlets work in harmony. The mycelium wraps around the roots of its host tree, some like one particular tree, some like a variety, once connected, it then provides the tree with nitrogen and receives sugars and nutrients in return.

What other mushrooms start with J?

K Kurotake

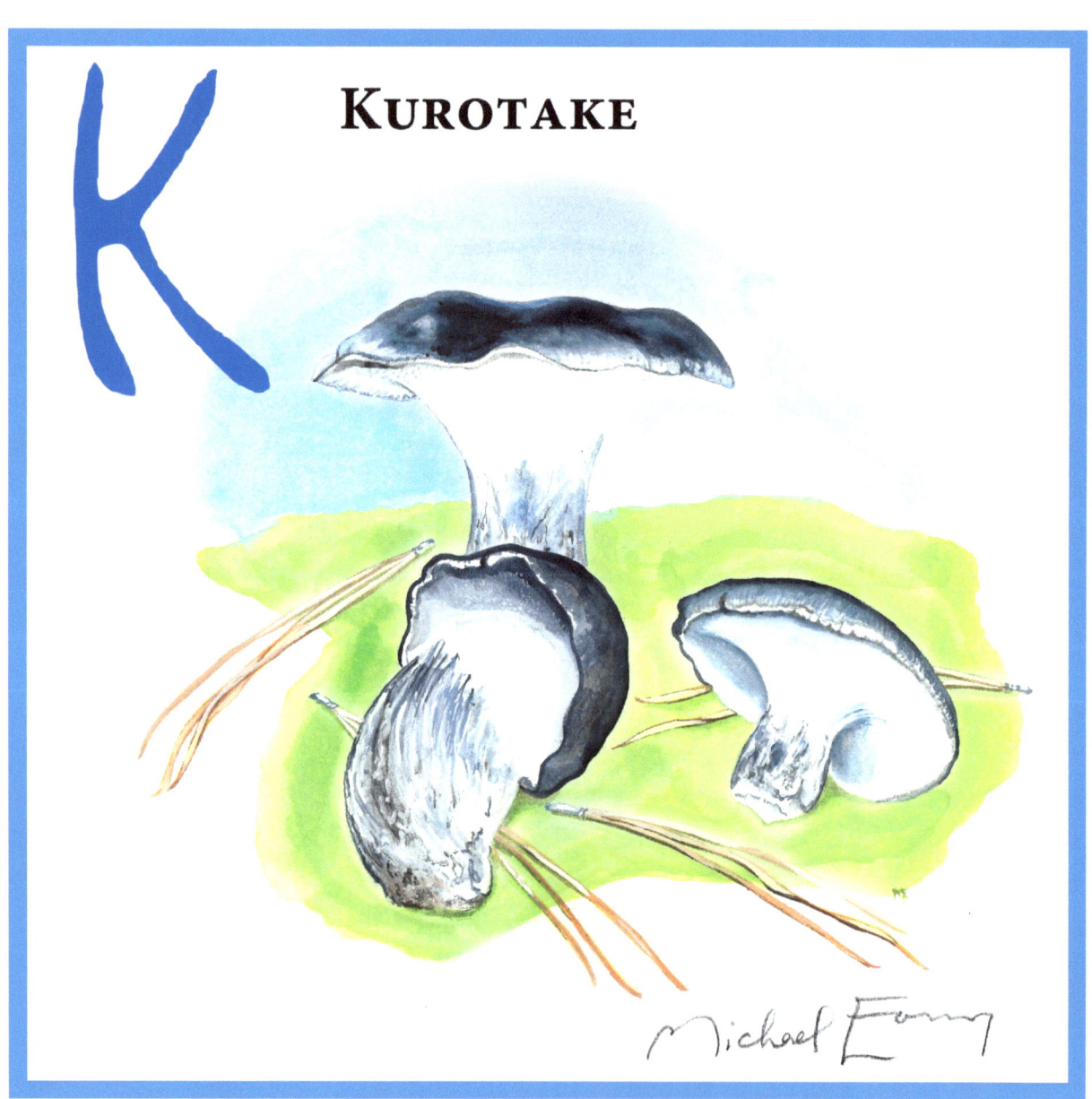

K is for **Kurotake**, Boletopsis grisea, B. leucomelaena

Kurotake mushrooms are popular edibles that, as their physical appearance and genus name suggest, resemble boletes. They are large, fleshy, with a greyish to blackish-brown cap with purplish tints, that is wavy, uneven and dry. It has pores like the boletus, that are white. Like the bolete, kurotakes bruise easily, darkening on contact. The thick, bulbous stem or stipe is white, and it too darkens upon touch. It is found from late fall to mid-winter in California's coastal and mountain forests. It's widely distributed but not common. Though the kurotake is bitter, this has not dampened its popularity. While it doesn't rival the Matsutake, it is highly sought after in Japan where it is soaked in brine for up to a month to remove the bitterness; boiling does not work. Another use for the kurotake is to thinly slice and dry it, this also removes the bitterness. It can then be added to meals or powdered and mixed with Kosher salt to make a spicy kurotake seasoning.

Cool fact: All those Latin names can be hard to get your head around. There's Boletopsis fayod and B. smithii, to name just a couple. I don't pretend to know all the phylum, class, order or family each mushroom belongs in. I'm not a mycologist, just a mycophagist. The common name will suffice to get you going and is often all you need to know. Try Boletopsis perplexa; Boletopsis means resembling Boletus fungi while perplexa means obscure or confused. Perplexing, right?

What other mushrooms start with K?

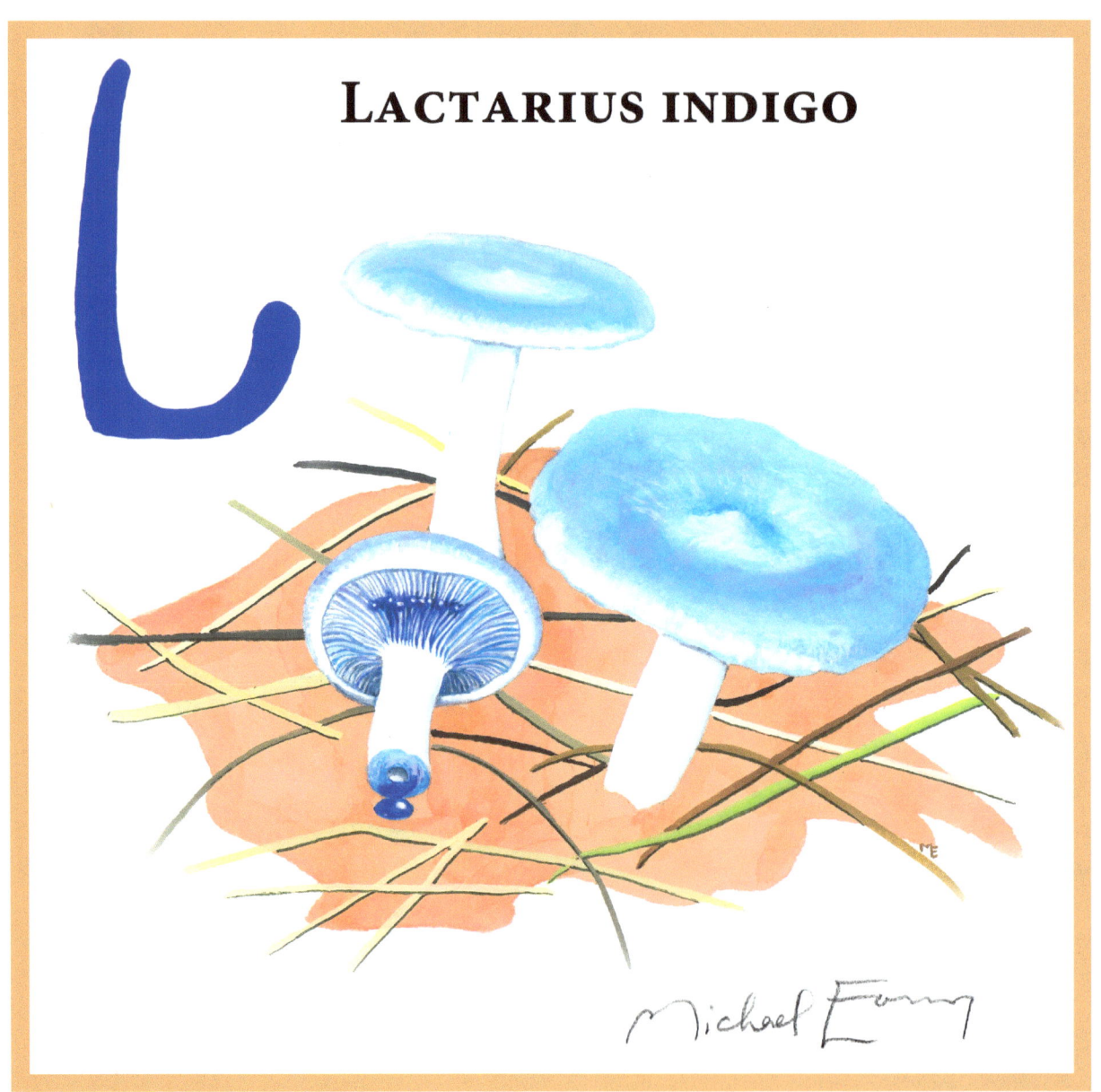

L is for ***Lactarius indigo***, Indigo milk cap, blue milk mushroom

Lactarius indigo is a striking and easily recognized mushroom. Though not common, it is wide-spread, from Virginia to Texas, along the Gulf coast down to Mexico, Guatemala into Costa Rica and Colombia. It also occurs in China and India. *L. indigo* is mycorrhizal, exchanging minerals and amino acids with a broad range of trees. They don't grow *on* the trees, rather, as noted under J, their mycelium interacts in a mutually beneficial way with the roots of the host tree. It's one of those agaric fungi, so look for the round cap that becomes vase or funnel-shaped, gills that taper into the stalk and of course, the bright, indigo blue milk or latex that oozes out when cut. 2" to 6" in diameter reaching 3" high. It can be found in rural markets in China, Mexico and Guatemala but you will probably have to pick your own in the United States. It is called a "superior edible" by some and "mediocre" by others. The Blue disappears with cooking, so you won't have a blue meal, though mixing it, thinly sliced, in scrambled eggs, will give you green eggs! There is an *L. indigo diminutirus*, (that means small), found in Virginia and Texas, a number of other *lactarius* that are bluish and naturally, some poisonous look-alikes. So, be cautious, as always.

Cool fact: There is an *L. salmoneus* named, like the indigo, for its milk which is bright salmon colored. Unlike its bright flashy cousin *L. indigo*, *L. salmoneus* is chalky white with some yellowish-brown stains, it keeps a low profile until it is cut or bruised, whereupon it shows its true colors.

What other mushrooms start with L?

M Morel

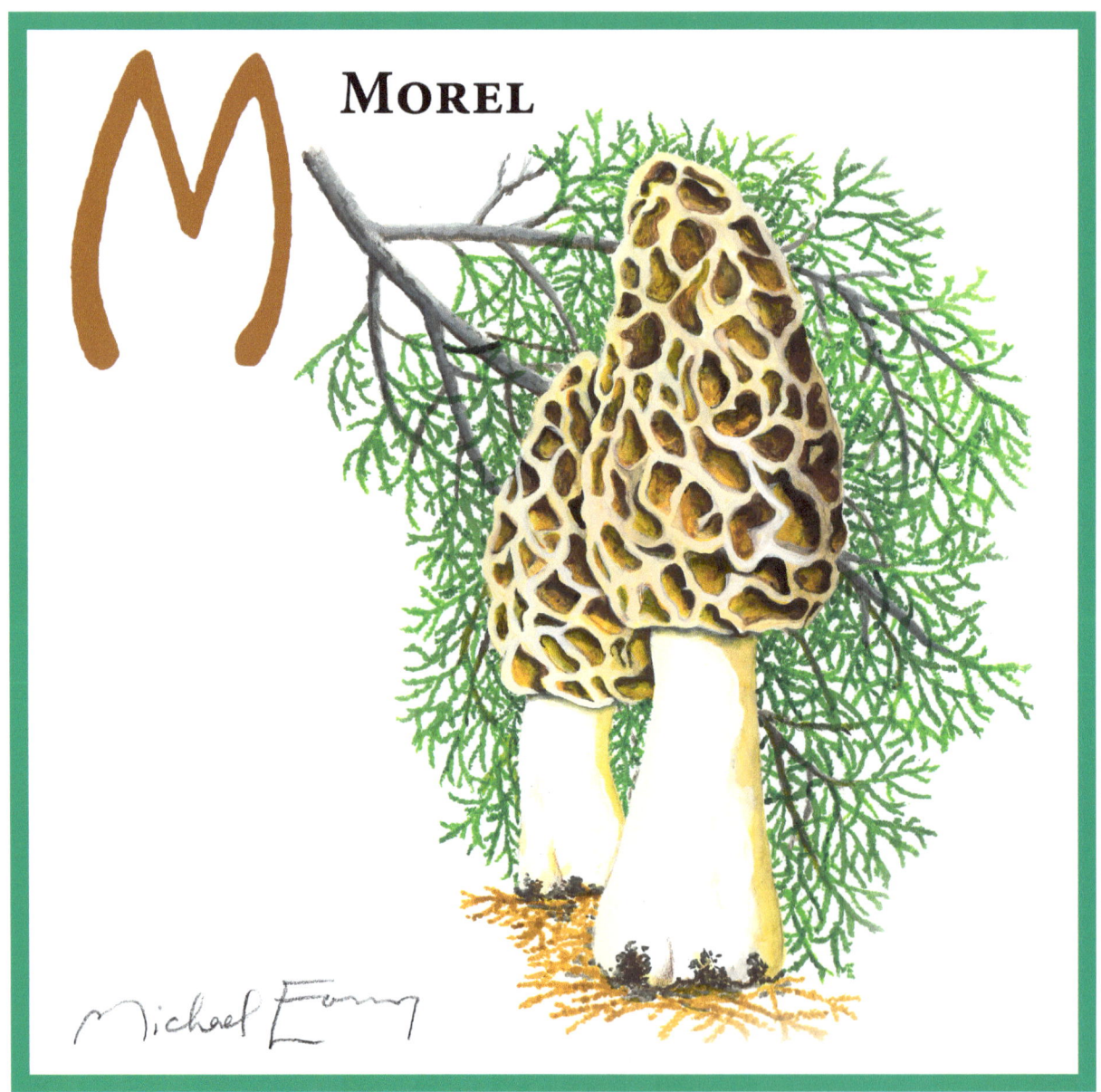

M is for **Morel**, *Morchella*

Morel mushrooms are considered by many to be the most delicious of all mushrooms. Luckily, it is also one of the easiest to identify. That said, there are also false morels and look-alikes. Personally, I don't think they really do look so alike and once you have identified a morel, I think you will agree. Worldwide some thirty morels exist. In the Texas Hill Country, three are most common, though the most prolific is the *Morchella esculenta*. Look for the tall cap that's rather like a pinecone in shape, pitted all over. Always cut the stem just above the ground, pulling the morel out of the ground will harm the underground mycelium from which the mushroom is flowering and may kill it. The clincher in identifying the morel is to slice it in half lengthwise. The morel will be completely hollow inside. They must be cooked before eating. Morels are toxic when consumed raw. The morel is rather fussy about its growing conditions, the soil has to be a precise temperature with just the right humidity. You might think that the controlled environment conditions of cultivation could solve that problem. Such efforts have not been too successful. Years may go by when no morels will appear in Texas but when conditions are right, they come up everywhere, out of rocks, in the sidewalk. I've even found them growing in streams! Then you can be picking morels for a month, beginning the first week of March. Some years fall can be like spring in Texas, causing fruit trees to blossom and there are tales of fall morels!

Cool fact: The toxin in raw morels is Hydrazine, the same thing as rocket fuel. Small amounts of hydrazine in tobacco smoke cause eye, nose and throat irritation, dizziness, headache, nausea, pulmonary edema, seizures and coma. Not to mention cancer.

What other mushrooms begin with M?

N

NIDULA CANDIDA

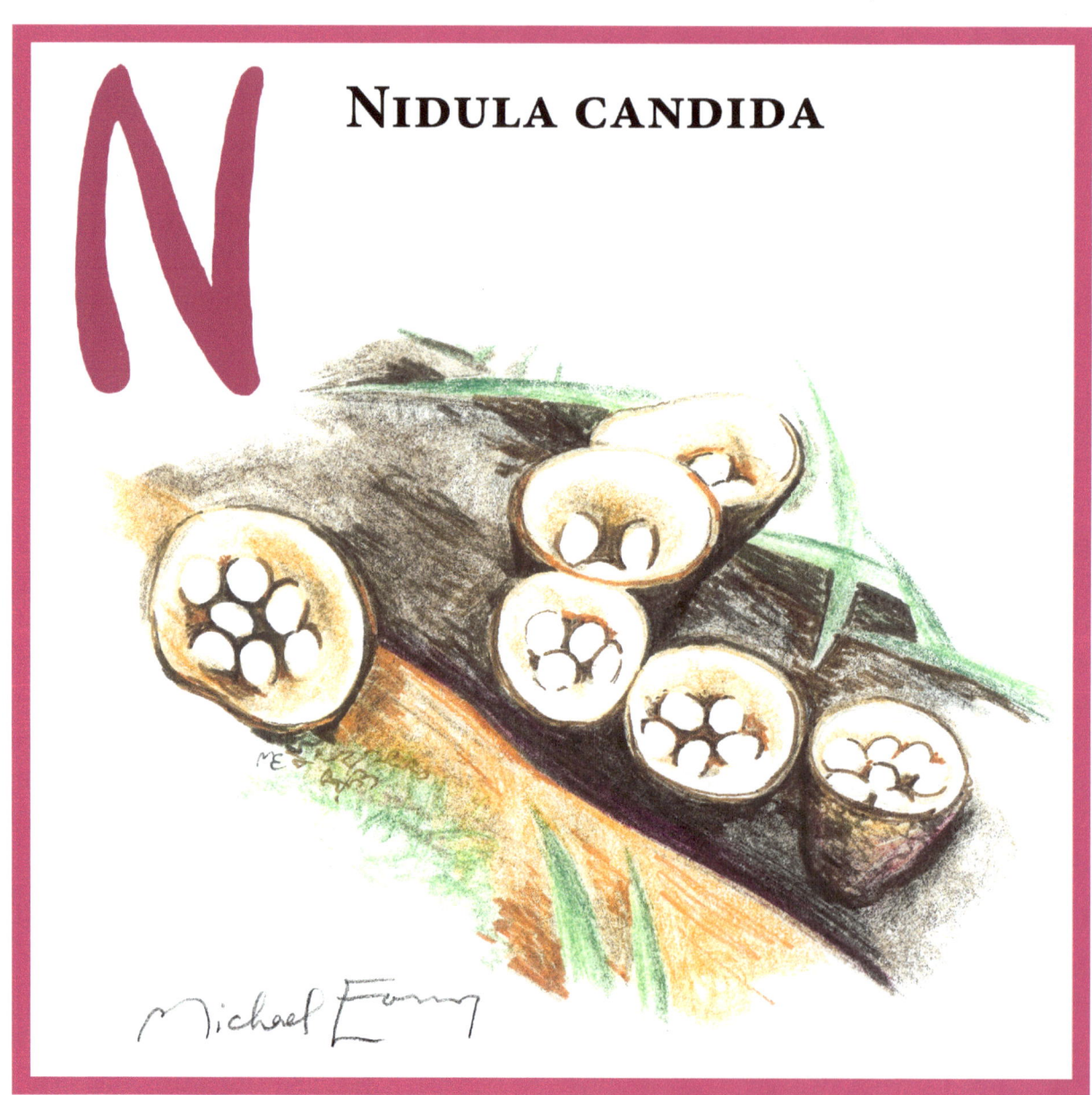

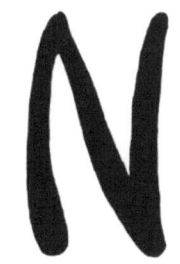 is for ***Nidula candida,*** Jellied Bird's Nest

Nidula candida is just one of the many bird's nest fungi that are quite common around the world. The candida is mostly found in the Pacific North West, though they are found in Louisiana and countries as diverse as New Zealand, England and Jamaica. They are very small and easily overlooked. Fresh mostly in summer or fall, they grow in clusters, mostly on decaying wood. Shaped like a flower pot *N. candida* has a shaggy grey-brown exterior. Color varies with species, and there are some bright orange-brown ones. The *niveomentosa's* shape is more like a mug, and they can fruit on the same spot for years. You might wonder where the bird's nest idea comes from, until the lid comes off and the 'eggs' sitting in a gelatinous goo are revealed. The lid, known as the epiphragm, prevents rain from entering the 'nest' until the eggs are ripe and ready to be dispersed. Nidulas are not edible and at their size would require a whole lot to provide a meal, anyway.

Cool fact: The Fluted Bird's Nest "eggs" are each attached to the cup by a hollow tube which contains a cord. As the egg flies out, propelled by a rain drop, the cord unreels. The cord is sticky so that, should it collide with a twig, it will wrap itself around until it is fully wound and the egg has contact with a potential food source. It's not over yet, though. It still needs another mycelia to 'mate' with, so only a tiny minority get to reproduce. There is another hope, small animals eat the mushrooms, and the still viable spores pass right through their systems and might yet wind up in a place where they can begin to grow.

What other mushrooms start with N?

O

Oyster mushroom

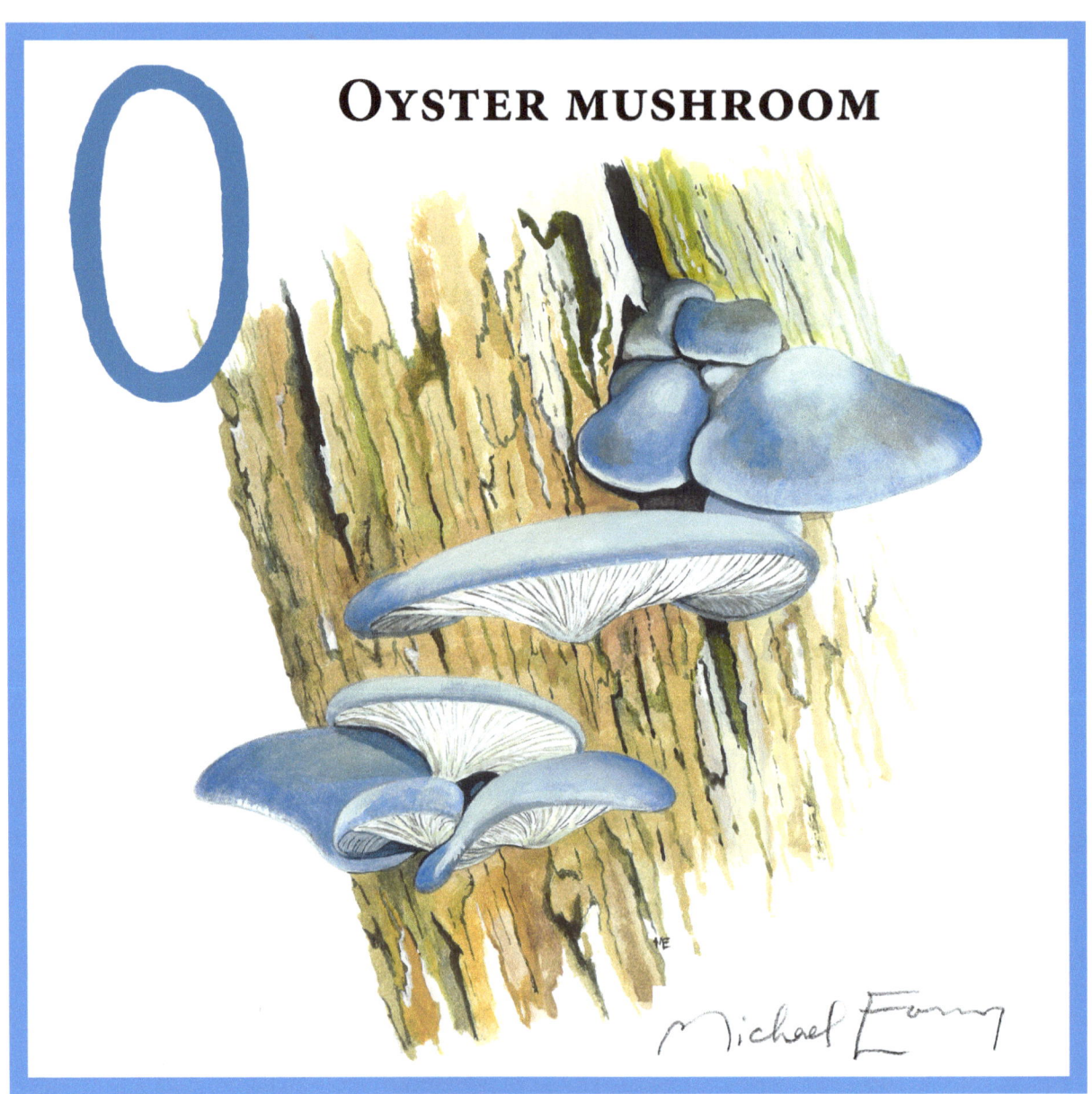

O is for **Oyster** mushroom

Pleurotus ostreatus, P. pulmonarius, P. populinus

Oyster mushrooms were first cultivated in Germany during WW II as subsistence food. Now one of the most popular cultivated mushrooms in the world, (it grows almost everywhere), in the wild it grows mostly on dead or dying hardwood trees. Pleurotus ostreatus is usually pale to dark grey, though other species can be blue, green, yellow or pink. The white gills under the cap extend down the short to barely existent stem which is off center so that the cap, starting out domed or rounded, can fan out from the tree as it ages, reaching up to 8 inches across. Extremely perishable, it should be used quickly, but don't wash the mushrooms until shortly before cooking (washing mushrooms is not generally recommended). This mushroom dries easily and can be used without rehydration. The oyster mushroom's name comes from the fact that in shape and color it resembles a freshly shucked oyster. It should be eaten cooked as it can cause allergic reactions when raw. The western jack-o-lantern and the ivory funnel mushroom are two toxic look-alikes to watch out for. Oddly, the Pacific Northwest of the USA is one place where P. ostreatus does not grow. There, P. pulmonarius and P. populinus fill in. The trees that the oyster grow on have died or are dying from something having nothing to do with the mushroom. In some places it is believed that the mushroom is killing the tree, but the fact is, the mushroom is decomposing the dead wood, completing the process of returning the tree's vital elements back into the ecosystem.

Cool fact: The oyster mushroom is carnivorous. Its mycelium eats nematodes and bacteria. An interesting article by Alister Bland at metroactive.com reports how the oyster mushroom is being used to clean up toxic oil spills.

What other mushrooms start with O?

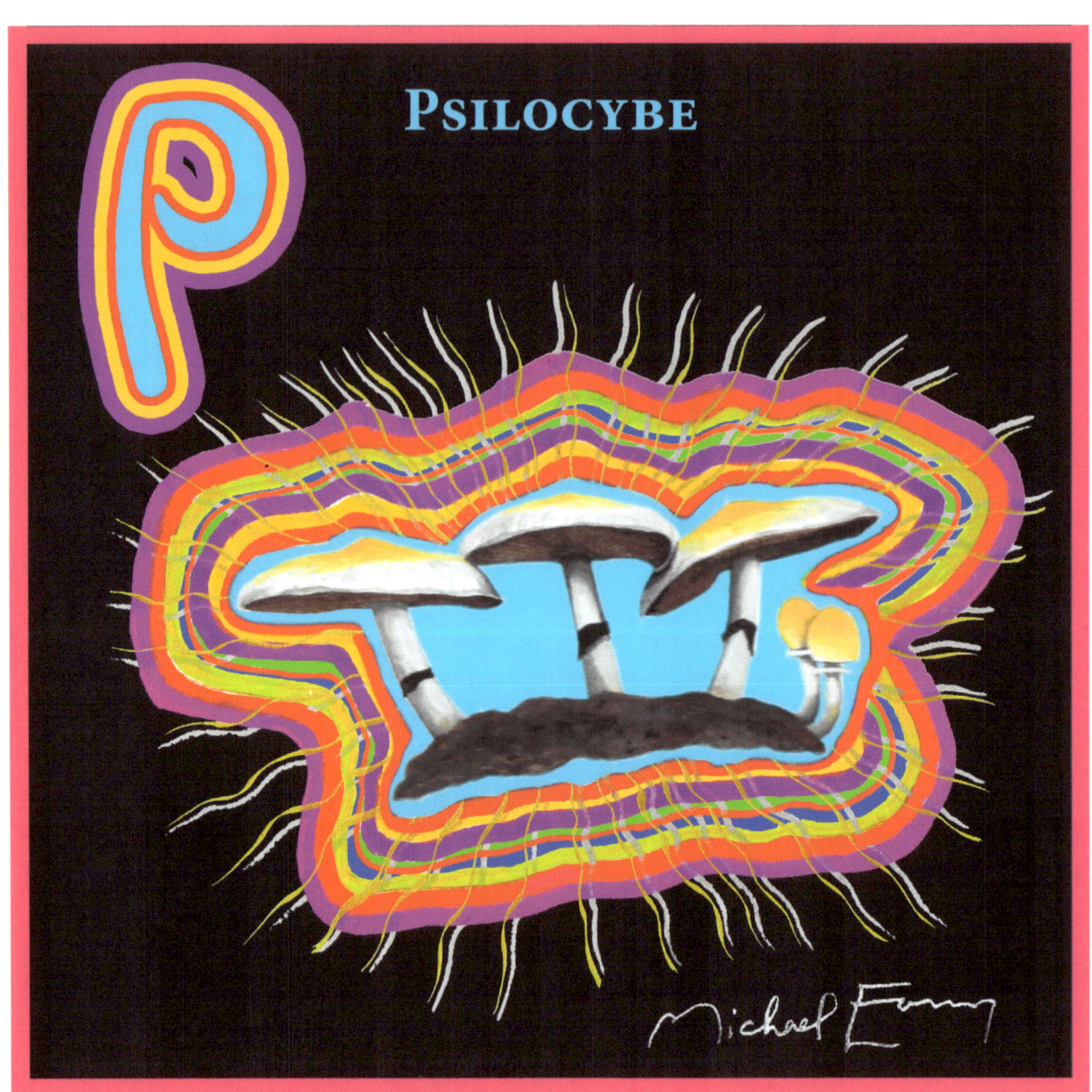

P is for **Psilocybe**, Magic mushroom

Psilocybe cubensis, is the most common of the psilocybe mushrooms. It's found in the Southeastern USA, Cuba (hence the name), and from Canada, down to northern South America, the subtropical Far East, including India, and parts of Australia. There are a number of psilocybe mushrooms that are psychoactive which makes their possession illegal in many countries. As with all mushrooms, be absolutely sure you know what you are picking before eating. Poisonous look-alikes can fool even the best. In most, if not all of the countries where psilocybe grows, native peoples use them in their religious ceremonies just as their ancestors did. Known as "Flesh of the Gods" to the Aztec, it was equally revered by the Nahua, Mixtec, Zapotec and Maya in Mexico as an aid in healing ceremonies and in communicating with the gods. Amateur mycologist R. Gordon Wasson took part in a ceremony conducted by a Mayan shaman in 1955 and wrote a book about it. Arguably, the book's publication set off the psychedelic revolution in the USA, which soon spread around the world.

Puffballs.

Puffballs are a particularly interesting member of the mushroom family. Except for the inedible ones, they have no visible stalk. They must be all white inside to eat, turning darker and tougher with age. The giant puffball can be bigger than a football and some are no more than a few inches in diameter.

Cool fact: The ancient Mexican God Tlaloc was the God of rain, the God of inspiration, and the toadstool God. Having been engendered by lightning, just as mushrooms were thought to be, it was only natural that Tlaloc preside over the ceremonial eating of psilocybe.

What other mushrooms start with P?

Q is for Quality mushrooms

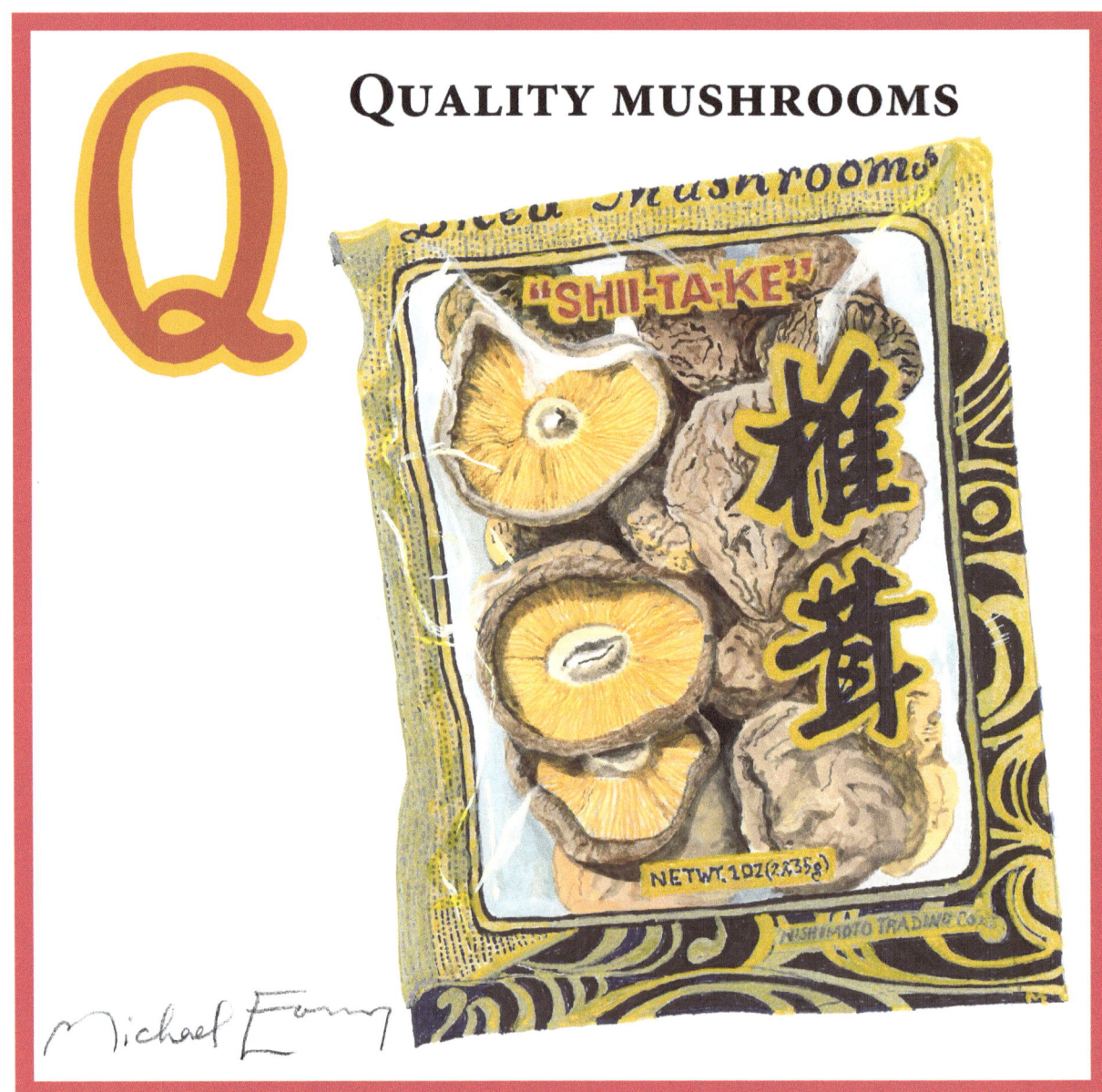

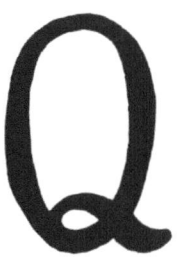 is for **Quality** mushrooms

Quality edible mushrooms are what the average mycophage is seeking. Why? Because a mycophage is someone or something that likes to eat mushrooms! While we are at it, a mycophile is someone that likes mushrooms. A mycophobe is someone who's wary or even afraid of mushrooms.

Quality mushrooms are all around us, though we may not notice them or appreciate all that they do for us. When I say mushrooms, I include yeasts, that give bread texture and flavor, and makes all the wines and beers; molds that ripen cheeses such as Roquefort, Brie and all the blue cheeses. Penicillin is another mold we are lucky to have, as it has saved lives and relieved the suffering of millions. Fungal products control bugs and weeds better than pesticides, and fungi are even used to control fungi. The USDA pesticide data program found residue of the fungal pesticide thiabendazole on more than half of tested store-bought mushrooms, so pick your own or buy organic. We have already seen how many mushrooms have medicinal properties and are now seeing products grown from mycelium used to make packaging, adding another environmentally friendly weapon to eliminate waste and to clean up our world. A fungus, *Aspergillus tubingensis,* newly found in a disposal site in Pakistan, can breakdown polyurethane! Some of the more delectable mushrooms turn up in these pages, but of course, there are many more and everyone has their favorites. Some are not much to look at while others are spectacular in size and color. Raw, cooked, pickled, powdered and mixed with liquids, all have their own distinctive taste and odor.

Cool fact: Enzymes derived from mushrooms are being added to some laundry detergents to make them clean better, saving water and energy.

Reishi

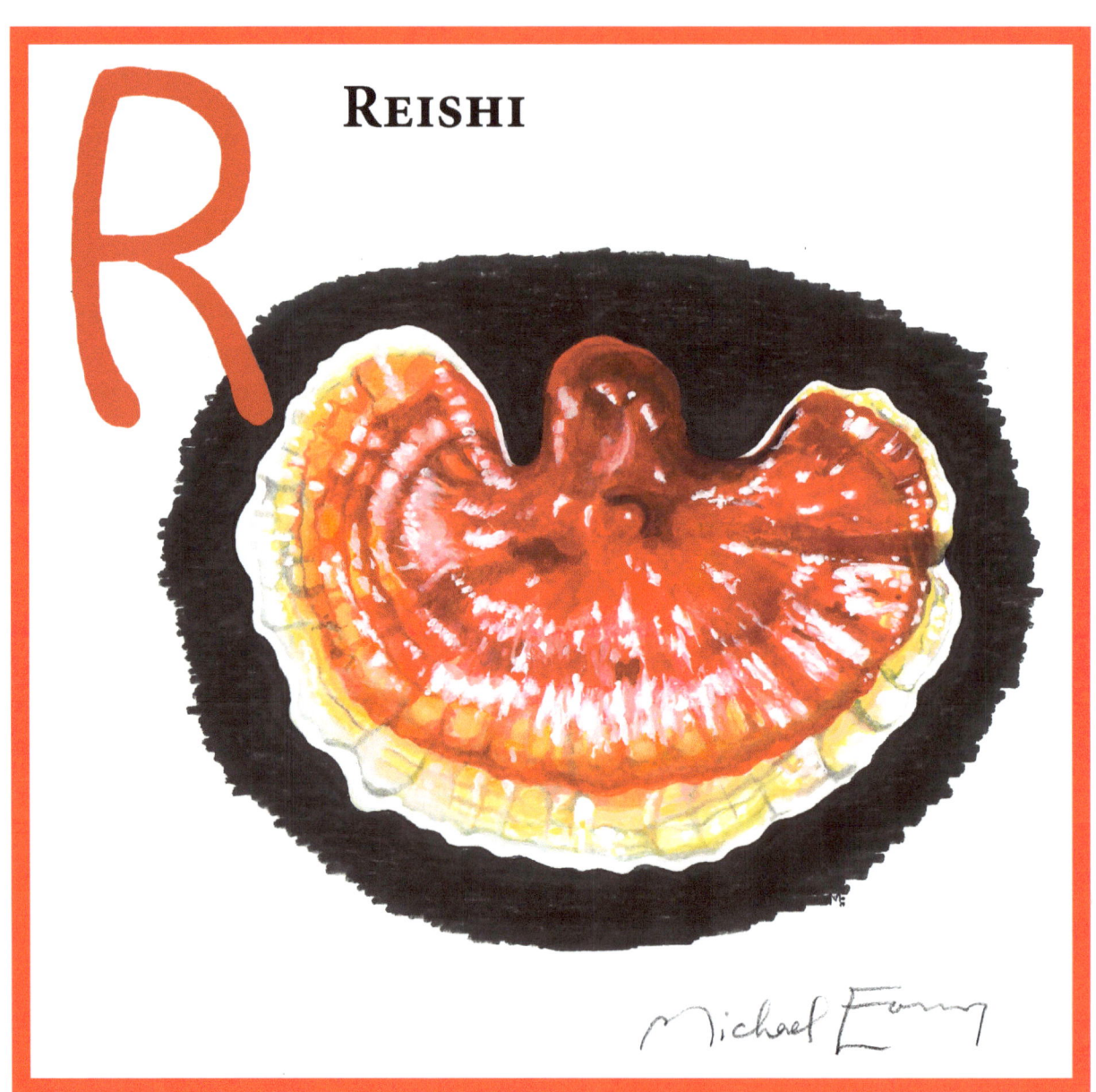

R is for **Reishi**, Ganoderma lucidum

Reishi is a shelf mushroom that can develop a stalk of considerable length. Whether it does or not appears to depend on the amount of carbon monoxide it is exposed to. Its Latin name *lucidum* which means "shiny" is in reference to the smooth, varnished look of the cap. Reishi has gotten a lot of attention in the west in recent years for its highly touted healing properties. Many studies have been carried out to try to determine what it is about reishi that accounts for the vast range of diseases as well as common ailments it cures or alleviates. All indications are that its ability to normalize and regulate the body's organs and functions is what yields the medical benefits. It is recommended as a regular general tonic, having no side-effects other than detoxification symptoms as the body is cleansed, symptoms that usually go away after a few days. If you are thinking you might try it, check with your doctor first. Reishi cultivation was developed in Japan where it is carried out on a large scale, though other countries including China and the USA have gotten into the act. Reishi comes in a variety of colors, but only the red and black appear to have any health enhancing effects with the red being number one. Apparently, it has always been rare in nature, such that, it was reserved strictly for royalty in Japan and China for thousands of years.

Cool fact: Known as Lingzhi (Ling 'divine' zhi 'fungus') in China, it is one of the oldest known mushroom medicines, having been used there in traditional medicine for over two thousand years. It was known as the 'plant of immortality'.

What other mushrooms start with R?

S Stinkhorn

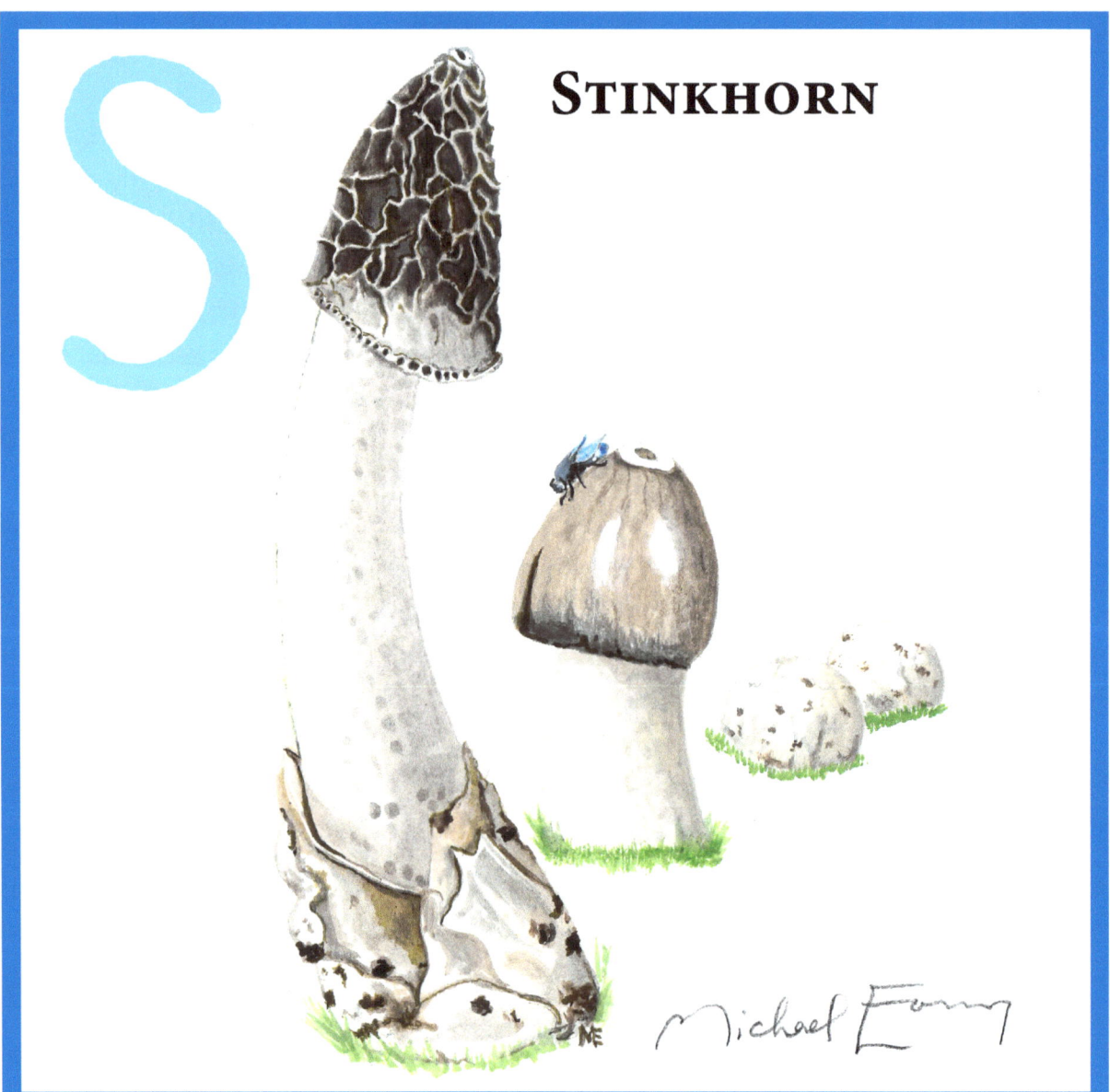

S is for **Stinkhorn**, *Phallus impudicus,* Phallaceae

There are several kinds of stinkhorns around the world. Those with a cap at the top of a stem have earned this mushroom the *Phallus* designation for very obvious reasons. Its other name comes from the fact that unlike other mushrooms, which release their spores into the air, this one produces a sticky slime on the top of its cap which attracts flies and other insects who carry the spores that are in the slime away with them after visiting. The slime stinks. Although some stinkhorns resemble morels, they come up in summer when you won't see a morel and, of course, they stink. Others in the family resemble tentacled or clawed sea creatures or take more bizarre shapes. Another of their distinctions is that they start from an underground "egg." Check out the *Phallus indusiatus,* known as the veiled lady, crinoline stinkhorn and bamboo fungus, sometime, and you will hardly believe your eyes. Unlike others in the family, this one is edible and has been used in Chinese medicine for centuries and yes, it stinks too.

Shiitake   S is for Shiitake, *Lentinula edodes*

Shiitake mushrooms provide many health benefits. It's called the "miracle mushroom", and the things that it is claimed to cure or protect one from are many. The Chinese have used it for over 6000yrs. It is the second most popular mushroom in the world. It is native to Asia, so you won't find it growing in the wild in the USA. However, they are now cultivated all over the world, so you could get some shiitake spores, some rotting logs and start your own mushroom farm.

Cool fact: Shiitake is Japanese, the "shii" being the name of the tree upon which it grows, although several other trees will work. "Take" is mushroom. (See the illustration under Q.)

What other mushrooms start with S?

T   Truffle

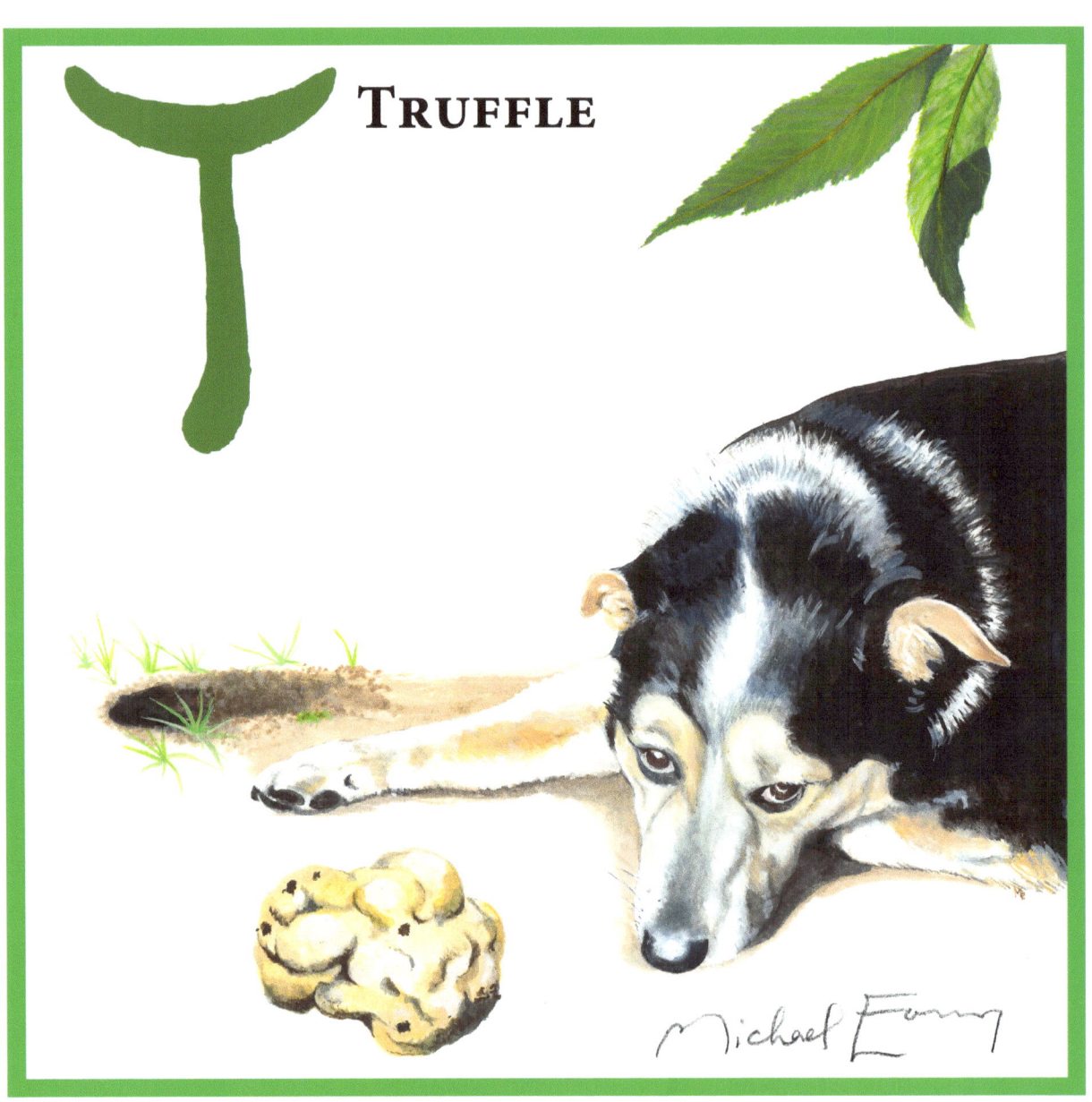

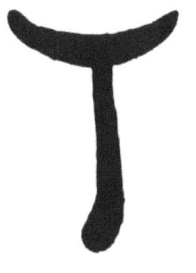 is for **Truffle**

Truffles are the fruiting bodies of fungi that grow underground near tree roots, their spores are distributed by fungivores, animals that eat fungi. Human harvesters use female pigs or dogs to find truffles. The pigs have a natural ability to find truffles but because they can harm the mycelia with their digging and because they will eat the truffle unless muzzled, their use has been prohibited in Italy. Trained dogs have no such problem. Truffles are the most expensive legally sold food in the world. There are people who pay very large sums in order to eat rare or endangered animals and plants. That they are hastening the disappearance of those species doesn't seem to bother them. Truffles are usually no more than a few inches in diameter. In 2010 a pair of white truffles, one of which weighed over a kilo, sold for $330,000.

Toadstool T is for toadstool

What are toadstools? I'm glad you asked. Some people think that mushrooms are the edible ones and the poisonous ones are toadstools. The fact is, there has never been a consensus. Dating back to the 15th century, when the words appeared, they have been interchangeable. In old German folk tales, toads were often portrayed sitting on a mushroom earning it the name, Krötenstuhl, toad stool in German. Aside from toads, fairies and elves are associated with toadstools and there are many tales and works of art depicting their relationships.

Cool fact: The Pecan truffle, *Tuber lyonia*, ranges from Northern Mexico to Canada. Also associated with oaks, hickories and other nut-bearing trees it was long considered a nuisance by pecan farmers, now truffle lovers will pay $160 per lb. for them at market.

What other mushrooms start with T?

Ustilago

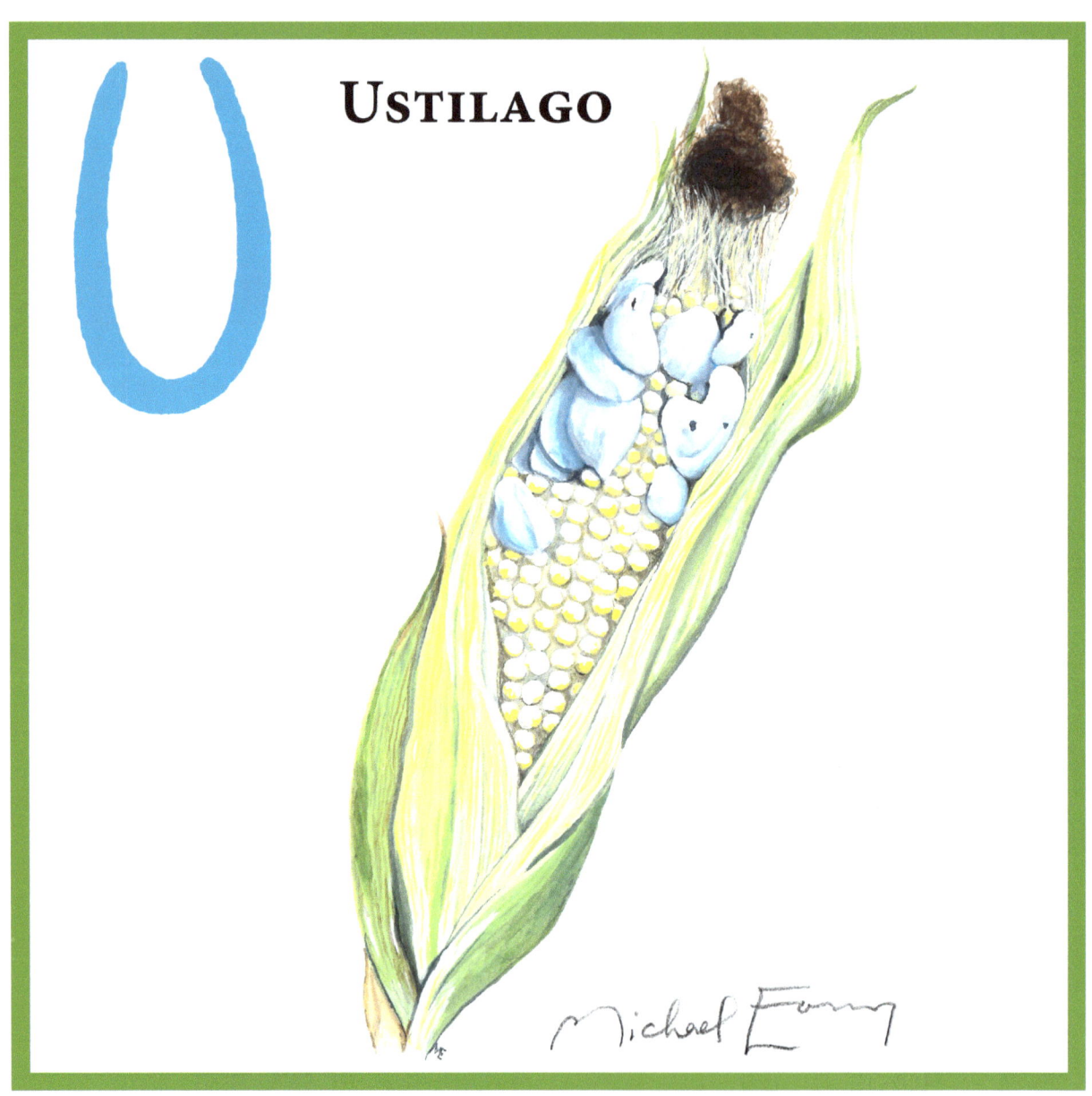

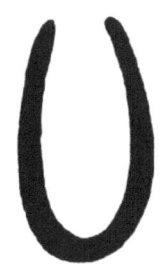 is for **Ustilago**

Ustilago maydis, Blister smut, Maize smut

Ustilago maydis is a smut fungus that infects corn. Since the use of herbicides seems to increase the disease, it is generally recommended that high density planting, heavy fertilizing and irrigation be avoided to decrease the need for chemicals. This is just as well, since this fungus is considered a seasonal delicacy and can be found at better Mexican restaurants under the name, "huitlacoche" (wheet-tla-KO-cheh). Cuitlacoche is the name given it by the Aztec. The Aztec liked it so much that they encouraged its growth on corn. Under normal conditions, huitlacoche is only available in July and August so, in order to keep up with demand, methods to produce it year-round are being developed.

Urnula criterium

U is for *Urnula criterium* The Devil's Urn

This little cup shaped fungus, usually black on the inside and grey outside, is found east of the Rockies in the spring. It grows on dead branches that are laying on the ground. Their appearance is a clue to morel hunters that the morel season has begun. It is considered edible but unpalatable.

Cool fact: Huitlacoche growing on corn changes the nutritional value of the corn for the better. It contains more protein than regular corn and the amino acid lysine, of which uninfected corn contains very little, abounds in that little smut, *Ustilago maydis*.

What other mushrooms start with U?

V Verpa

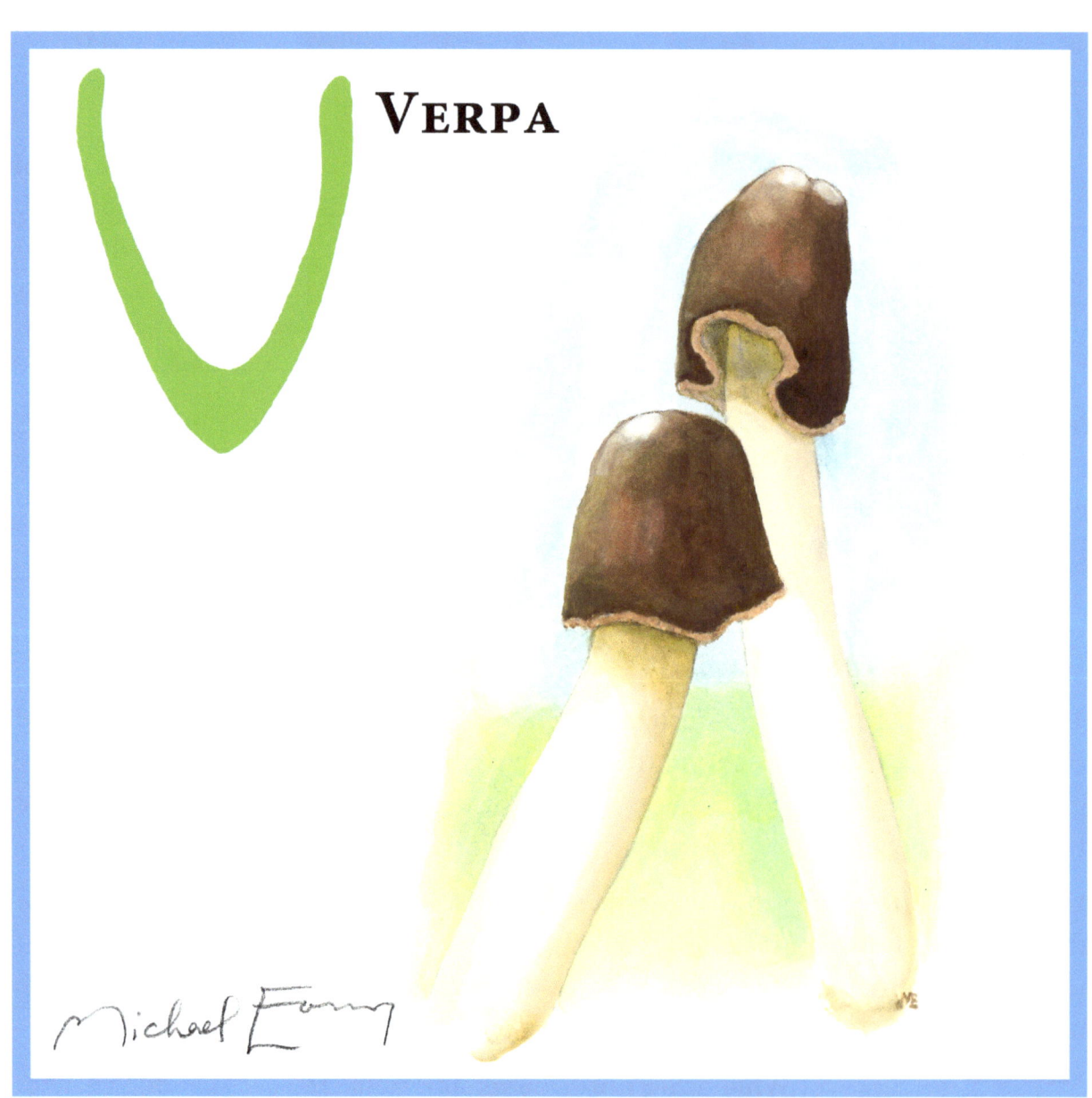

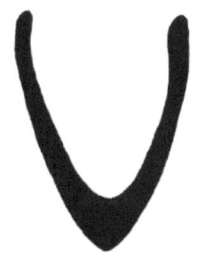 is for **Verpa**, False morel

Verpa mushrooms, particularly the *Verpa bohemica*, are known as false morels. Personally, I don't think they resemble morels to any great extent but just in case you encounter a mushroom you think might be a morel, here are some things to look for. The cap is only attached at the top of the long stem with the bottom hanging free, skirt-like, at the bottom? Not a morel. The stem is not hollow but contains cotton-like membranes? Ditto. The wrinkled folds of the verpa cap is very different from the pitted, sea sponge look of the morel, though I realize that few people these days are familiar with natural sponges, due to over harvesting by mankind. Manufactured sponges look more like the underneath of bolete caps. *Verpa conica* is more likely to be smooth, with the same free hanging cap. Both verpas are considered edible, though, if you decide to try them, parboiling in lots of water, which is discarded, then eating only a little at first is recommended. Drying them first or only eating the caps are other suggestions. There are reports of poisoning in susceptible individuals, you never know if you might be one. Yellowish brown to reddish brown, they usually appear before the morels in the spring but overlap in time and habitat. Another false morel to watch out for is, *Gyromitra esculenta*. It has a heavily wrinkled, veined, brain-like cap. It comes in various colors, from reddish to dark purplish-brown. Follow the same precautions if you plan to try one. Though potentially deadly, it is still sold as edible in some parts of Europe.

Cool fact: The *Verpa bohemica* was first described by Julius Vincenz von Kromholz, a Czech mycologist. It has gone through a number of name changes over time, *Ptychoverpa bohemica* is favored in Europe. Bohemia is now part of the Czech Republic.

What other mushrooms start with V?

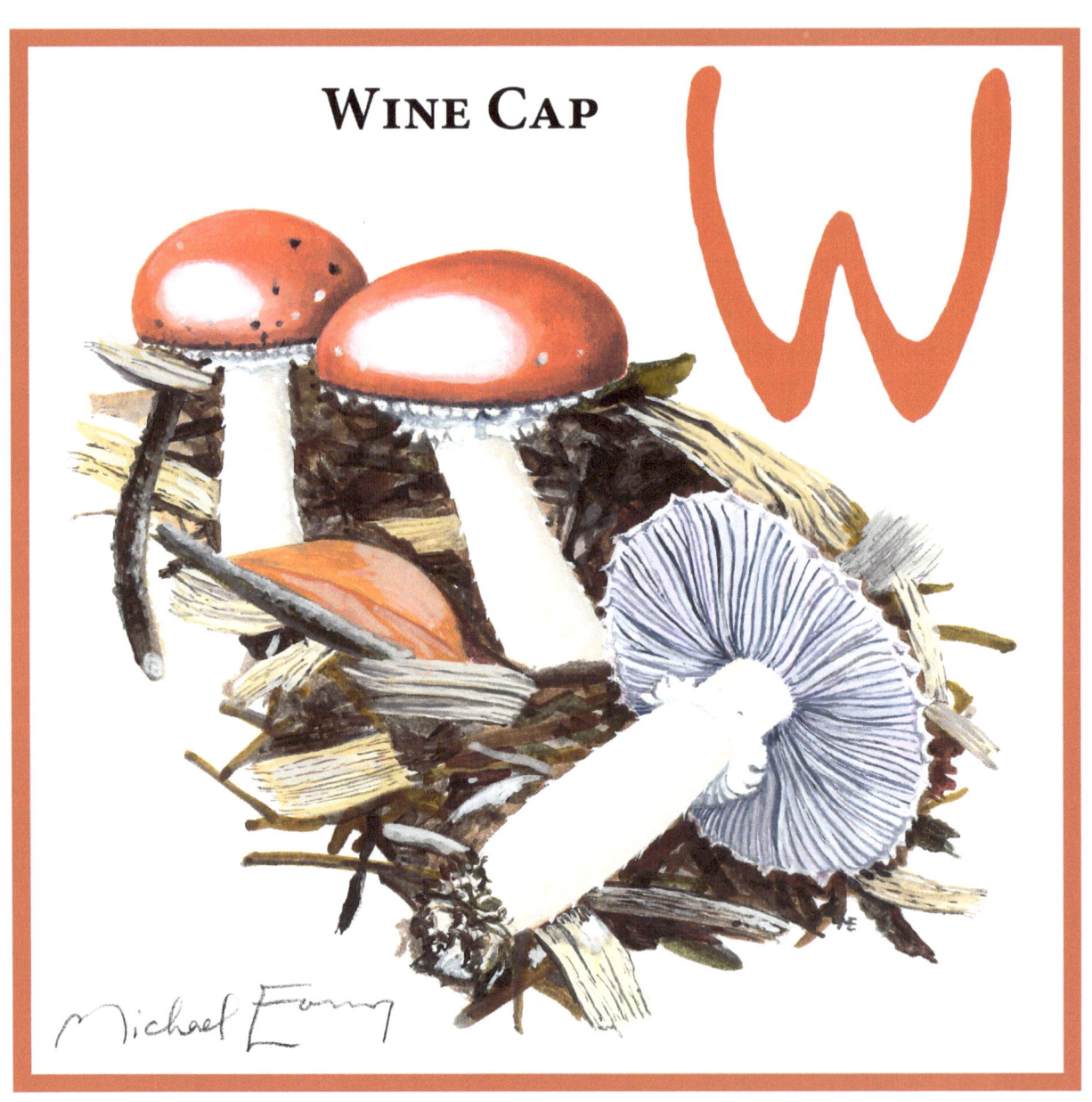

W is for **Wine Cap** *Stropharia rugosoannulata,* Burgundy mushroom, Godzilla mushroom

Wine caps are more agaricas in the Strophariaceae family and another nematode eater. If you have a nematode problem in your garden, you might want to employ some of these mushrooms. There are around 160 nematode eaters with different methods of getting their prey. Some species of fungi live inside the nematode from the start, some trap them with adhesive strands or nets while others attract nematodes by pretending to be nematodes. The wine cap puts out a toxin that stuns them, then it eats them. Enough about that. What you want to know is, how do I recognize it, and can I eat it. The answer is, they are pretty easy to identify, they have no poisonous look-alikes and they are considered 'choice'. They can be found in the wild from early summer to autumn. The reddish-brown or burgundy convex cap is a little sticky young, it flattens with age, the gills that attach to the stem start out pale, turn grey then dark purple-brown, the spore print is purple if you decide to check that, and the stem has a ring around it that can look like a cogwheel. The wine cap is easily cultivated and may be found in farmers' markets. That Godzilla tag comes from the fact that it can get pretty big. The cap can get off-white to yellowish, up to a foot in diameter and five pounds in weight. By that time the stem is not good to eat but the cap might be and the whole thing is certainly good for bragging rights.

Cool fact: While the *Stropharia rugosoannulata* and some blue green agarics are choice edibles, the genus *Stropharia* is generally not considered good to eat. The Louisiana State Act 159 prohibits the growing, selling or possession of the *Stropharia* spp.

What other mushrooms start with W?

Xylaria polymorpha

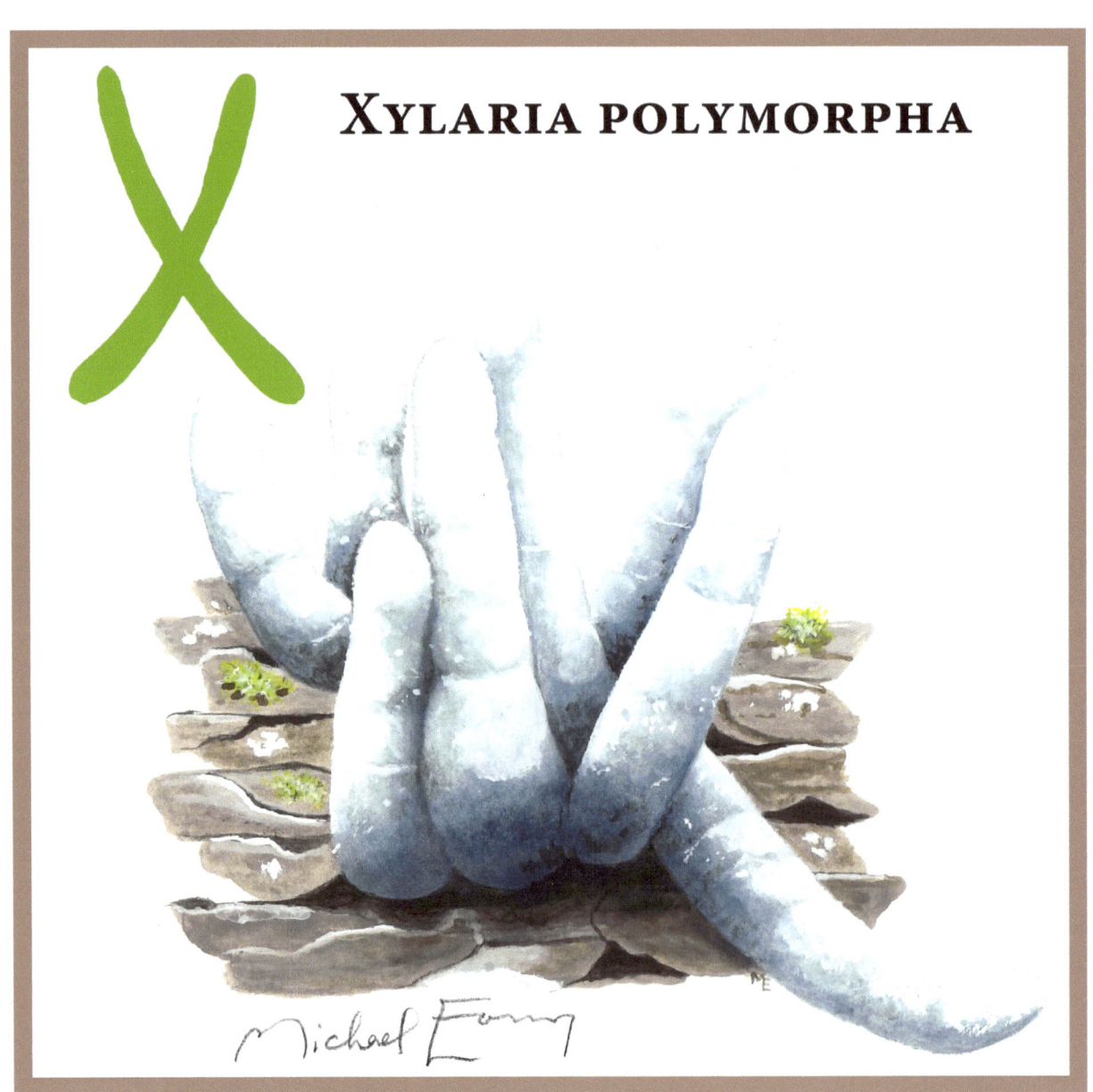

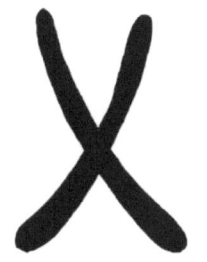 is for ***Xylaria polymorpha*,** Dead Man's Fingers

Xylaria polymorpha lives on a wide range of dead and decaying trees, since it is helping in the process of decay. "Finger-like" or clustered to form "hand-shaped" bodies, these grey to greyish-brown mushrooms develop a carbon-like crust as they age. Unlike most mushrooms, they can live for months or years, releasing spores all the while. Young specimens have a light-colored tip, and sliced they have a surprising white interior ringed with black dots that are the spores waiting to be released. The upper two thirds are tender and can be eaten raw or cooked. There are lots of opinions about eating raw mushrooms, most being against it. I have also seen advice against eating gilled mushrooms because those are responsible for most mushroom related deaths! However, that would deprive us of many choice edible mushrooms. If you are feeling adventurous, eat small amounts over a period of time. This won't tell you if they will harm you in the long run, but you will know if you are allergic. Thinly sliced pieces can be made more edible by putting them in an acidic mix, like in ceviche, otherwise, just cook them. Being small to start with, cooking does render them down, so you might just need a lot of them. As we have seen with so many fungi, the Chinese used *Xylaria* medicinally centuries ago, and it continues to be used for depression and sleep deprivation. There are some plants and parts of a crab known as Dead Man's Fingers, but it's not likely you would mistake them for *Xylaria polymorpha*.

Cool fact: It has been found that wood treated with *Xylaria longipes* becomes a 'mycowood', which has been used to make violins that have the acoustic properties of a Stradivarius, such that even Stradivari himself might not be able to tell the difference if he heard one played.

What other mushrooms begin with X?

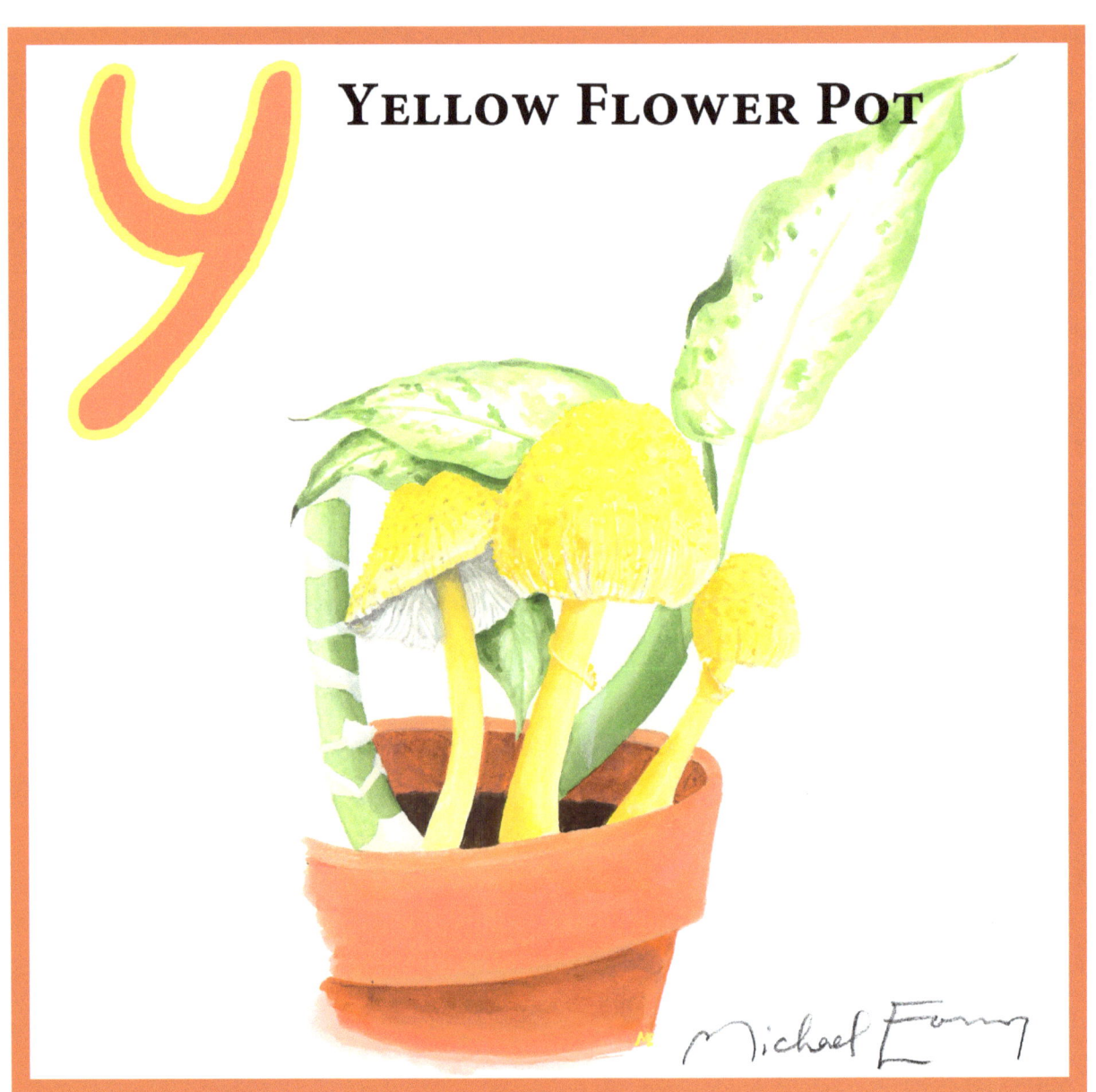

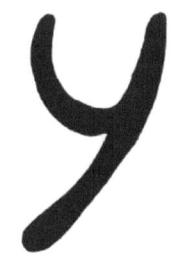 *is for* **Yellow Flower Pot**

Leucocoprinus birnbaumii, Lepiota lutea

Yellow flower pot mushroom hunting requires no special clothing, boots, equipment, travel or a packed lunch. They grow right there in your own home or greenhouse. If you have house plants, it's quite possible you have seen these mushrooms pop up in the flower pot. If you bought the potted plant or potted it yourself, the soil or mulch you got at the store was very likely already infected with spore or mycelia that were just waiting for the right conditions to fruit. Your tender care and hot weather was just what they needed. As the name implies, it is bright to pale yellow, can get a few inches tall, has gills that do not attach to the stem which will likely have the remnants of the partial veil attached in the form of a ring. The cap is covered in scales or dots. It won't harm your plant, just don't you, your kids or pets eat it. If you are a mycophobe, or just don't want mushrooms growing in your house, your best bet is to totally replace the soil. Picking the mushrooms before they deposit more spores might help, but if mycelium is in the soil more mushrooms will grow. Otherwise, just enjoy that dash of color and another mushroom to add to your list. Leucocoprinus birnbaumii is not the only mushroom that might turn up in potted plants, but it is the most common.

Cool fact: In 1785, this species was first named Agaricus luteus by an English mycologist. Unfortunately, another fungus already had that name. In 1839, a Czech mycologist named it for the greenhouse inspector in Prague who saw it in a greenhouse. The inspector's name was Birnbaum. That name stuck, although in some reference books you will see Lepiota lutea, yellow parasol, parasol mushroom and more names attached.

What other mushrooms start with Y?

Z

Zowie

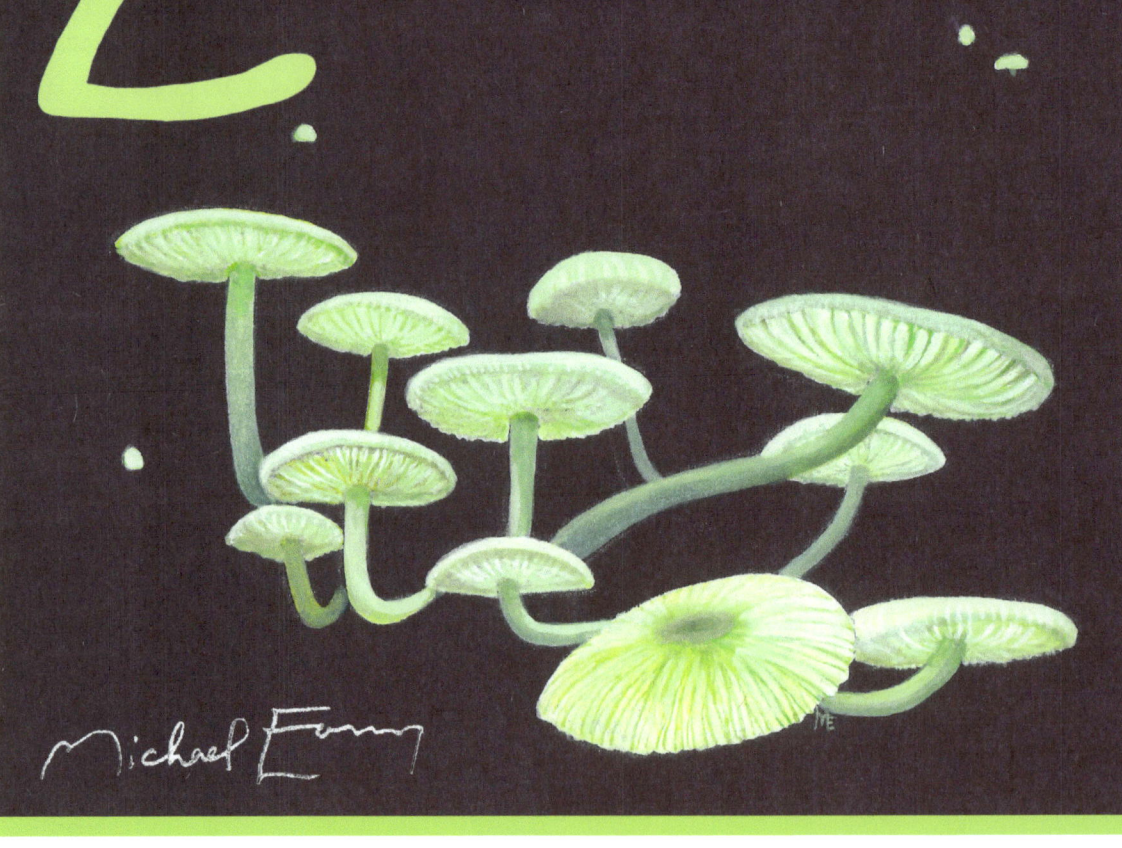

Z is for **Zowie**, Zowee, Wowee Zowee

Zowie! Or wowee zowee! As defined in Merriam-Webster's dictionary: "used to express astonishment or admiration". If these two words don't express your feelings about mushrooms after reading thus far, perhaps some of the following unusual, odd and downright bizarre facts about mushrooms will.

First off, there is bioluminescence. Known as foxfire, the light emitted by some fungi is created by the interaction of luciferase and luciferin. It is believed that the light acts to attract insects that spread the spores. Though usually dim, the light can be bright enough to read by.

It has been contended that religion came about from the use of mind-altering drugs and also that civilization itself came about thanks to the use of psychedelics. In *The Sacred Mushroom and the Cross* (1970), John Marco Allegro lays out a strong argument that the story of Jesus Christ is actually a hidden coded message for a secret cult whose members used the psychoactive *Amanita muscaria*.

The California Red-Backed Vole lives in northern California and western Oregon, feeding mainly on false truffles. The truffle spores are distributed by the vole. You can guess how. The vole is an essential part of the ecosystem. When clear-cut forest is cleared of all dead wood and trimmings, the truffles stop fruiting, the vole population dies off and newly planted trees do not thrive. Why is the Northern Spotted Owl on the threatened species list? They depend on old growth forest and the red-backed vole forms an important part of their diet. Don't mess with Mother Nature!

Zelleromyces is a species of fungus in the Russulacaea family and falls under the genus *Lactarius*.

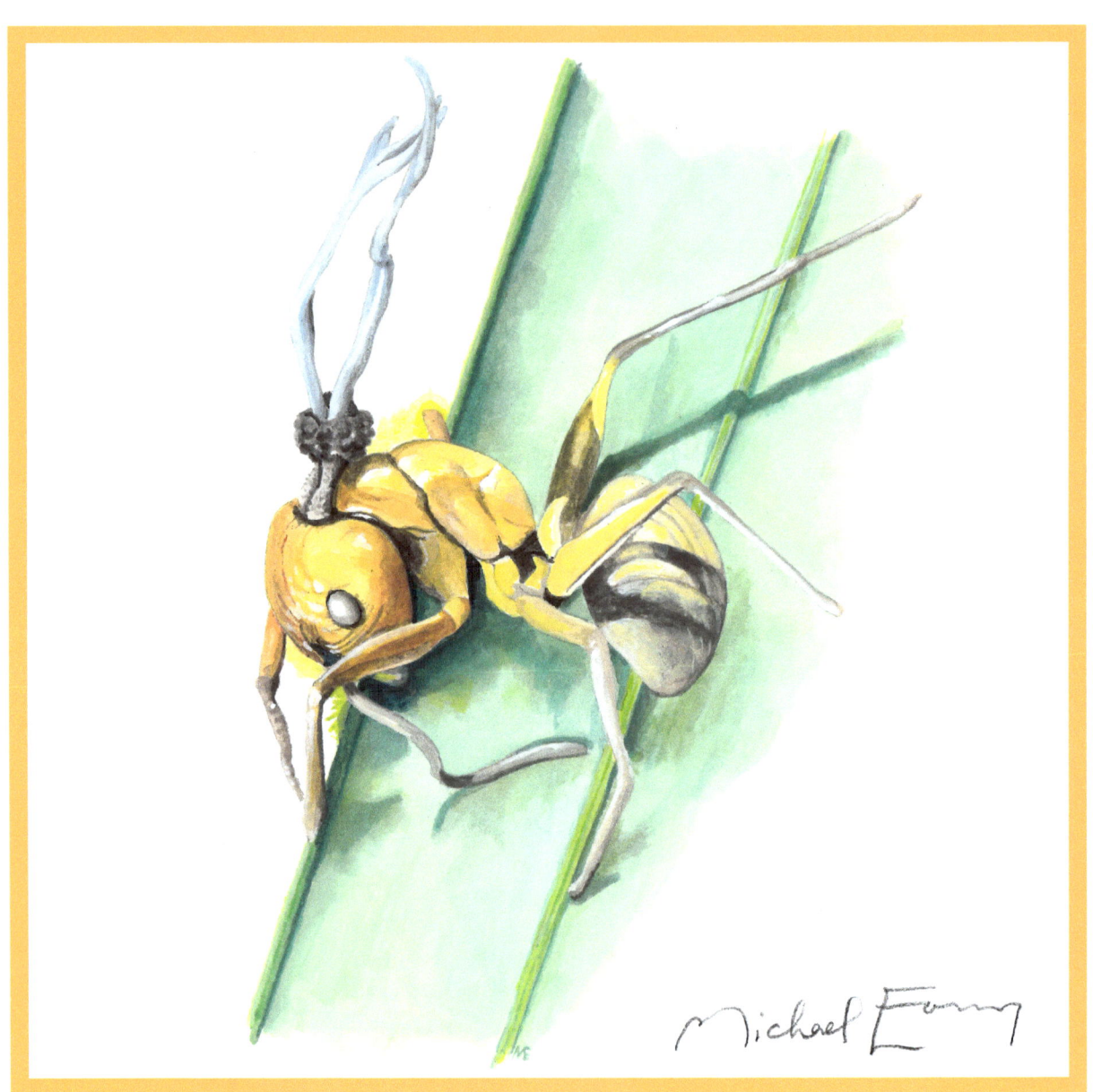

Bonus Mushroom

Here is one more mushroom to elicit your astonishment or admiration.

Cordyceps   *C. sinesis C.unilateralis Ophiocordyceps unilateralis*

Cordyceps is another fungus used in Chinese medicine for centuries for its medicinal and nutritional benefits. In recent years, studies have found it to have definite cancer fighting abilities besides increasing energy levels, fighting stress and fatigue, increasing immunity to viruses and promoting longevity. What's not to like? Well, there is a darker side to Cordyceps. It is a parasitic fungus, but rather than attaching to trees, each species selects one particular insect to infect. The O. unilateralis favors an ant in the Brazilian rain forest. Once a spore penetrates the ant, it takes control of the ant's muscles and moves it to do what it needs rather than what the ant needs. Under the guidance of the fungus, the ant climbs down from its normal habitat, finds a leaf or stem at a specific height, facing a specific direction with the right temperature and humidity. There, it bites down and after a few days, dies. After another few days, the fruiting body of the fungus emerges from the head of the ant, grows and releases its spores. The whole cycle starts over when some unsuspecting ant walks by. In order to protect the colony, if one ant's behavior seems odd, another ant will carry it off and dump it where it can do no harm. Part of the fungi's job is to stop ant colonies from growing too large and upsetting the balance of nature. Oh yes, there are some cordyceps that infect other cordyceps.

Cool fact: When members of the Chinese women's track team set multiple world records in 1993, the question was asked, "How did they do that?" Turned out they were drinking a brew that included *Cordyceps sinensis* which grows on a caterpillar. It's now very popular among athletes.

More A to Z Mushrooms

A. Artist Conk, Albatrellus flettii, Arrhinia epichysium
B. Blewitt, Bearded tooth, Black trumpet
C. Coral-pink Merulius, *Calocybe carnea*, Comb Tooth
D. Dryads saddle, Deer mushroom
E. Earth stars, Eyelash cup, Eastern Cauliflower
F. *Flammulina velutipes*, Fried Chicken Mushroom, Fawn Mushroom
G. *Gautieria monticola*, Garlic Mushroom, Green Cracking Russula
H. *Helvella lacunose*, Hairy Rubber Cup, Haymakers Mushroom
I. Indian Pipe, Indigo Milky,
J. Jelly Bellies, Jelly Baby
K. Kriegeria alutipes, King Bolete
L. Lobster Mushroom, Lantern stinkhorn, *Lactarius laccata*
M. Man on Horseback, *Mycena pura*,
N. Nidula candida, Nectria cinnabarina, Naucoria vinicolor
O. Oldman of the woods, Orange Pinwheel Marasmius
P. Polyporus elegans, Peziza ellipsospora, Pinesap
Q.
R. Reddening Lepiota, Ringless honey Mushroom
S. *Seta Shimeji*, Shrimp of the Woods, Scarlet Cup
T. Thelaphora palmata, Turkey tail
U. Urnula cratorium, Urstalina deusta
V. Volvarina speciosa, Vascellum pretense
W. Witch's Hat, Wolf's Milk Slime, *Weraroa cucullata*
X. Xanthoporus, Xeromphalina campanela
Y. Yellow Patches
Z. Zelleromyces

Bibliography

Mushroom-expert.com
Medicalnewstoday.com
Psychedelics.com
Psychedelicgospels.com
Ancientorigins.net
Americanmushrooms.com
www.fungi.com
www.youtube.com
psychonautwiki.org
www.mushroom-appreciation.com
theforagerpress.com
www.virtualmuseum.ca
Allegro, John Marco 1970. *The Sacred Mushroom and the Cross.* Hodder and Stoughton (eight editions by other publishers)
Wasson, Valentina and R. Gordon. 1957. *Mushrooms, Russia and History.* Pantheon Books
Krieger, Louis C.C. 1967. *The Mushroom Handbook.* Dover Publications
Milagro Mata. 1999. Macrohongos de Costa Rico. INBio
Bone, Eugenia. 2011 *Mycophilia.* Rodale
Lincoff, Gary. 2010 *the complete Mushroom Hunter.* Crestline
www.metroactive.com
draxe.com
www.first-nature.com
Wikipedia.com
TomVolkFungi.net
www.doctorfungus.org
wildfood.com UK

BBC
Scientific American
www.mycoweb.com
www.fungicopia.com
bib.ge/soko/fungi-species
www.treehugger.com
www.sciencedaily.com
www.britannica.com
svharvest@wordpress.com
AlfieAesthetics
doorofperception.com

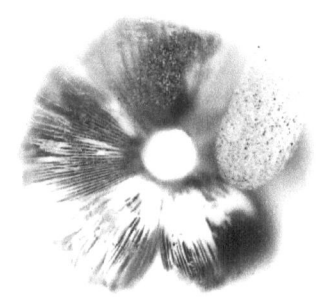

Recommended viewing

The Magic of Mushrooms. BBC Television
Paul Stamets' TED talk, "6 ways mushrooms can save the world"

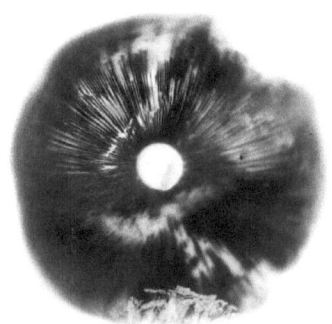